ENCYCLOPAEDIA OF INDIAN GOVERNMENT: PROGRAMMES AND POLICIES

ENCYCLOPAEDIA
OF
INDIAN GOVERNMENT:
PROGRAMMES AND POLICIES

Vol. 17

Steel and Mines

Edited by

Satish Tiwari

ANMOL PUBLICATIONS PVT. LTD.

NEW DELHI - 110 002 (INDIA)

ANMOL PUBLICATIONS PVT. LTD.
4374/4B, Ansari Road, Daryaganj
New Delhi - 110 002

Encyclopaedia of Indian Government: Programmes and Policies

First Edition, 2000
ISBN 81-261-0515-1 (Set)

PRINTED IN INDIA

Published by J.L. Kumar for Anmol Publications Pvt. Ltd., New Delhi - 110 002 and Printed at Mehra Offset Press, Delhi.

Contents

Preface

Encyclopaedia of Indian Government: Programmes and Policies contains authoritative information on about fifty departmental policies and their future developmental programmes.

Organised to be completed in 40 volumes, this gigantic work covers Agriculture; Atomic Energy; Chemicals and Fertilizers; Coal; Commerce; Communication; Culture; Defence; Education; Environment and Forests; External Affairs; Finance; Food & Consumer Affairs; Food Processing Industries; Health and Family Welfare; Home Affairs and Internal Security; Human Resources; Industry; Information and Broadcasting; Labour; Law, Justice and Company Affairs; Non-conventional Energy Sources; Ocean Development; Parliamentary Affairs; Personnel, Public Grievances and Pensions; Petroleum and Natural Gas; Planning and Programme Implementation; Planning and Statistics; Posts and Telegraphs; Power; Rural Development; Science and Technology; Social Justice and Empowerment; Space; States Affairs; Steel; Steel and Mines; Sugar and Edible Oils; Surface Transport; Textiles; Tourism; Urban Development; Water Resources; Women and Child development etc.

Based on the information derived from authoritative sources, this work contains authentic facts and figures. I am deeply beholden to all the scholars whose writings are cited or substantially made use of in the present work. I am also thankful to Anmol Publications Pvt. Ltd. for undertaking publication of this encyclopaedia. I am solely responsible for shortcomings in presentation of matter.

Encyclopaedic in nature, this will prove a dependable reference work for scholars and academics besides those appearing for different competitive examinations.

—Satish Tiwari

Preface

1

Introduction

Demand and availability of steel

Total demand for finished steel including domestic requirement and for exports in 1997-98 was 24.51 million tonnes. Against this, the domestic production during the year was 23.37 million tonnes leaving a gap of 1. 14 million tonnes which was met through imports. During 1998-99 the demand for finished steel (Carbon & alloy steel) is 26.73 million tonnes. Against this, the availability is projected at 27.73 million tonnes of finished steel.

Production of steel

Total production of finished steel in 1997-98 was 23.37 million tonnes. India is the 10th largest steel producing country of the world. Main producers contribute 10.44 million tonnes (45%) and secondary producers 12.93 million tonnes (55%). During 1997-98, the share of main and secondary producers in the total production of finished steel has remained more or less the same as in 1996-97.

Production of finished steel (carbon & alloy steel) in the four integrated steel plants of SAIL and its subsidiaries during 1997-98 was about 7.21 million tonnes registering a decline of 1.66% over last year.

Production of finished steel in Visakhapatnam Steel Plant (VSP) was 1.62 million tonnes in 1997-98 as against 1.45 million tonnes in 1996-97 registering an increase of

14.5%. T1SCO produced 1.90 million tonnes of finished steel in 1997-98 as against 2.00 million tonnes in 1996-97 registering a decrease of about 5% over last year.

Steel consumers council

The Steel Consumers Council was constituted on 31.1.1986 under die Chairmanship of Minister for Steel and Mines to provide a forum for interaction between Government and various sections of steel consumers. The main function of the council is to advise and assist the Government in matters relating to availability of steel materials, quality and the market trend in the iron and steel industry in the country. The last meeting of the council was held at New Delhi on 30.6.1998.

Steel industry

Steel Authority of India Limited (SAIL)

Performance of SAIL

The production of Saleable steel in the four integrated and special steel plants of SAIL for 1997-98 was 9.043 million tonnes as against 9.24 million tonnes in 1996-97. During the year 1998-99 (Upto September, 1998) production of saleable steel was 3.95 million tonnes against the target of 4.35.

IISCO

Production of saleable steel in IISCO, a subsidiary of SAIL in 1997-98 was 0.315 million tonnes as against 0.338 million tonnes in 1996-97. During 1998-99 (upto September, 1998) IISCO has produced 0. 145 million tonnes of saleable steel as against the target of 0. 159 million tonnes.

Working Results of SAIL

During the year, SAIL has achieved a turnover of Rs.14624.07 crores (Previous year Rs.14114.01 crores). The profit before tax at Rs.148.59 crores (Previous year Rs.588.03 crores) is after providing for interest of

Rs.1553.76 crores (Previous year Rs.1179.48 crores) and depreciation of Rs.794.86 crores (Previous year Rs.690.70 crores). After providing for Minimum Alternate Tax (MAT) of Rs.15.60 crores (Previous year Rs.75.86 crores), the Net Profit after tax is Rs. 132.99 crores (Previous year Rs.515.17 crores).

Major projects of SAIL

Capital Schemes

There are three steel plants where modernisation works were in progress during the year viz. Durgapur Steel Plant, Rourkela Steel Plant and Bokaro Steel Plant. SAIL has incurred a capital expenditure of Rs. 1955 crores during the year on fixed assets and capital work-in-progress, which has been primarily financed through borrowings from external sources. The latest position of the modernisation work in these plants and progress of major capital schemes in Bhilai Steel Plant are given below :

Durgapur steel plant

The modernisation of Durgapur Steel Plant (DSP) has been completed during the year. Major thrust was given on stabilisation of production and achievement of rated capacity. Benefits have started flowing in and are expected to increase further in future years. Production has picked up and has shown a growth of 5 per cent in Hot Metal, 9 per cent in Crude Steel and 14 per cent in Saleable Steel as compared to previous year.

Rourkela steel plant

At Rourkela Steel Plant (RSP), the various global and indigenous packages under Phase-II Modernisation are in the final stages of completion. The balance works in modification of Hot Strip Mill and Reheating Furnace of Hot Strip Mill is progressing. Trial production has started at SMS-2- Continuous Caster at RSP.

Bokaro steel plant

At Bokaro Steel Plant (BSL), major production facilities of Modernisation like both Continuous Casting Machines, Steel Refining Unit and Coiler-4 have been installed. Trials of Coiler-3 are under progress. Balance works for Mill proper are nearing completion, Modification of Reheating Furnace-3 to Walking Beam Furnace, and Coal Dust Injection system of BF-4 are under progress.

Bhilai steel plant

At Bhilai Steel Plant (BSP), Modernisation of Rail & Structural Mill (Stage-I Phase-I) has been commissioned. Oxygen Plant-II expansion and Twin hearth Furnace No.4 are in the final stages of completion. Work in Sinter Plant-3 and Cold Dust Injection system for BF No.6 are in progress.

With completion of modernisation schemes, substantial improvements are likely to take place in terms of techno-economic parameters, particularly, specific energy consumption, coke rate etc. besides better quality and increase in production capacity of saleable steel.

As a part of Government's initiative for development of North-East, a Hot Dip Galvanishing Line of annual capacity of 40,000 tonnes is being set-up at Dagaon, Assam for which site activities have started.

Rashtriya ispat nigam limited (Visakhapatnam Steel Plant)

VSP had fixed a target of 3.4 million tones of Hot Metal, 2.92 million tonnes of Liquid Steel, 2.58 million tonnes of Saleable Steel for the year 1998-99. During the first half of the year inspire of sluggish international market and unfavourable domestic market conditions VSP has achieved production of 1.52 million tonnes of Hot Metal, 1.26 million tonnes of Liquid Steel and 1.10 million tonnes of Saleable Steel which represents target fulfillment of 91%, and 87% respectively. This corresponds to 4% growth in Liquid Steel and Saleable Steel over Apr-Sep'97. The production of Billets, Bars and MMSM products have registered a growth of 2%,13% and 28% respectively over the corresponding period of last year. There has been improvement in the production of the value added steel from 114605 tonnes during Apr-Sep'97 to 118534 tonnes during Apr-Sep'98.

Electric arc furnace industry

It may be noted that during the licensing days, whereas steel production through the integrated route was reserved for the public sector, EAF units were being sanctioned. However, only very small capacities were being considered. And it was only in Sept., 1990 that capacities upto 1 million tonne were made eligible for sanction.

Presently, there are 187 electric arc furnace based steel plants in the country with an aggregate capacity of 10.67 million tonnes per annum. Of these, as many as 143 units with an aggregate estimated capacity of 5.34 million tonnes are reportedly closed. Various reasons such as rising cost of inputs, increasing electricity tariffs, shortage of power, shortage of finance etc. are believed to be responsible for this, underscoring the forces of change sweeping the steel sector.

Production of Ingots/concast billets by EAF units, which are reporting their production to the office of the Development Commissioner for Iron & Steel, during 199798 was 4.33 Million tonnes. The above figures do not include production of steel by the casting units registered with erstwhile DGTD.

Induction furnace industry

During 1997-98 there were about 922 Induction Furnace Units with a capacity of 9.2 million tonnes. However during the year it is estimated only 733 units were in operation. The capacity utilisation of the IF Units was only about 55%. The total production of the IF Units was estimated to be around 4.42 million tonnes.

Alloy and stainless steel industry

The Alloy/Stainless Steel industry contributes about 7-10% of the country's production of finished steel. During 1997-98 the production of Alloy/Stainless Steel was about 1.65 million tonnes which was about the same as last year.

Iron ore mining industry

Production of Iron Ore (including Concentrates) during the year 1997-98 was 73.45 against 68.17 million tonnes showing an increase of 7.7% than the previous year. Statewise production figures indicate that Madhya Pradesh was the chief iron ore producing State accounting for 25% of the total production during 1997-98, followed by Karnataka with 21%, Bihar 19%, Goa 18% and Orissa 16%. The remaining production would be from Andhra Pradesh and Maharashtra.

The performance of the two Public Sector Iron Ore Mining Companies viz : National Mineral Development Corporation Limited (NMDC) and Kudremukh Iron Ore Company Limited (KIOCL) was as under:

National Mineral Development Corporation Limited (NMDC)

During the year 1997-98 NMDC produced 14.59 Million Tonnes of Iron Ore and 30596 carats of diamond. For the year 1997-98, the Company paid a dividend of 25% on the equity capital amounting to Rs.36.34 crores, which was the eighth year in succession for payment of dividend.

In view of the increasing demand for Bailadila Iron Ore, two new Iron Ore Mining Projects are being undertaken in this region at Deposit No. 10/ 11 A and 11 B, the later in the joint Sector. Each of these Projects is designed to produce 5 million tonnes run-of-mine (ROM) Ore.

Kudremukh Iron Ore Company Limited (KIOCL)

During the year 1997-98, the Company recorded a Gross Margin of Rs.142.50 crores and a net profit after tax of Rs.81.81 crores against a target of Rs.125 crores (gross margin) and Rs.74.10 crores of net profit respectively. The Company paid a dividend of 3.50% of the paid up capital amounting to Rs.22.81 crores in 1997-98. The performance of KIOCL has been hampered by severe power cuts imposed by the Karnataka Electricity Board (KEB).

Sponge iron industry

Sponge iron is a metallic product produced by direct reduction of high grade iron ore or iron ore pellets in the solid state. Also known as Direct Reduced Iron (DRI) or Hot Briquetted Iron (HBI), it contains a large percentage of metallic iron. India is the second largest Sponge Iron producers in the world. This is a substitute for steel melting scrap used mainly in the electric steel making and in BOF processes. The indigenous availability of metal scrap is low and large quantities have to be imported in order to meet indigenous demand.

The growth of sponge iron specifically during the last five years in terms of capacity and production has been substantial. The installed capacity of sponge iron increased from 1.52 million tonnes per annum in 1990-91 to 6.06 million tonnes per annum in 1998-99. The production has increased from 0.9 million tonnes in 1990-91 to 5.31 million tonnes in 1997-98. The production of sponge iron has been reported to 2.64 million tonnes during April-September, 1998.

Pig iron industry

The pig iron industry profile is constantly undergoing changes with more mini blast furnace units in the private/ secondary sector coming up in the post liberalization era. The contribution of private/ secondary sector units, from only 8% during 1991-92 has increased to 48% in 1996-97, and further to 50% during the period 1997-98. The secondary sector units are also producing foundry grade pig iron including low sulphur and low phosphorous grades. During 1997-98,3.39 million tonnes of pig iron was produced against the projected demand of 2.9 million tonnes.

Ferro alloy industry

Ferro alloys are essential additives in steel making used for imparting desired properties to steel. The product mix of ferro alloy industry mainly consists of Ferro Manganese (Fe Mn), Ferro Silicon (Fe Si.) and Ferro Chrome (Fe Cr.) -called the Bulk ferro alloys. There are 35 large and medium size units (including four 100% EOUs) with an installed capacity of 1.3 million tonnes. The production of Ferro Alloys during 1997-98 was about 7.91 lakh tonnes which was 14% more than the previous year.

Refractory industry

Refractories are the primary materials used in the internal fining of industrial furnaces and are classified on the basis of chemical composition into Acid Refractories, Basic Refractories and Neutral Refractories. With the technological changes in the steel industry, the major thrust has been on economising on the use of the materials and improving technology in each area of operation/ process where refractories are being used. In general, it can be said that all these improvements have resulted in lowering specific consumption of refractories per tonne of steel. The production of Refractories during

1997-98 was 7.09 lakh tonnes which was 7.4% lower than the previous year

Management information system

The Computerised Management Information System (MIS) developed for Department of Steel with the assistance of National Informatics Centre (NIC) is functional in the area of Accounting and Budgeting Section Activity Monitoring System, Industrial Entrepreneurs memoranda System, VIP References Monitoring, Public Grievances Monitoring and Monitoring of Steel Production and Supply, Imports/ Exports, Duties, Prices, apparent consumption and category-wise production. A Local Area Network of about 50 nodes has been established by NIC in the Department for resource and information sharing among the various user communities in the Department. An attempt is being made to setup Internet by computerising Work-Flow & providing Web enabled applications in the Department on Local Area Network (LAN). Pentium based computers have been provided to senior officials in the Department. Software Standardization has been done by providing Office Automation Suit in Windows environment to ensure compitability among the Computer Systems provided with End-users. A Five-year IT Plan has been prepared for the Department in which 2 to 3% budget has been earmarked for providing computers, software development and training to the users in the Department. All the computers on LAN have been provided browsing and E-maii facility on Internet. Various in-house training programmes on LAN operations, E-mail & browsing operations on Internet and Windows-based Office Automation Suits have been organised by NIC Computer Centre in the Department from time to time.

Research and development

Both Public and Private Sector Iron and Steel plants continued their Research and Development activities to solve their plant specific problems and also to develop new processes and products. Emphasis was on improving the quality of the steel products, utilization of wastes and reduction of energy consumption as well as cost of production.

In pursuance of the decision of the Cabinet to spend upto Rs. 150 crores per annum for Research & Development efforts in the iron and steel sector, Government has set up an Empowered Committee to approve Scientific Research Programs and to provide overall direction to the research efforts on the iron and steel in the country. The Committee is working under the Chairmanship of Secretary, Department of Steel and includes representatives of major steel producers and other experts in the field. To service the committee's its secretariat, Research & Technology Mission is being set up.

Energy conservation

Iron & Steel Plants , both in public and private sectors continued to give thrust on the reduction in the consumption of energy. Introduction of coal dust injection in the blast furnaces; mixed gas firing in stoves of blast furnaces; on fine ceiling of steam, blast and gas leakage; introduction of fuel efficient burners; optimisation of combustion and modification of thermal regime in different shops of SAIL's plants have resulted in substantial reduction in energy consumption.

TISCO have also taken various measures for reduction of energy consumption like higher carbon monooxide (CO) yield, higher usage of by-product gases, lowest specific petro fuel consumption, introduction of rich CO gas firing system in Sinter Plant resulting reduction in energy consumption.

At Essar Steel Ltd., a good amount of developmental work has been going on for energy conservation like hot discharge of DRI, change of reformer fuel, retrieving power from turbo expander, decreasing tap to tap time at EAF etc.

Ferro Alloy Corporation (FACOR) is using hot charge mix directly during the reaction in the production of low carbon ferro chrome which helps in reduction in specific power consumption and also helps in increasing production of the alloy.

Environmental management and pollution control

The Iron & Steel Plants have drawn up short term and long term action plans for expeditious achievement of Pollution Control norms, wherever these have not so far been achieved. The Environment Laboratory Group of RDCIS, SAIL provide services to steel plants in the field of specialised statutory assessment of air, water and noise in steel plants and mines and also development and transfer of methodologies, Air and water pollution control, and Water and solid waste management.

VSP has been according high priority for maintaining a very clean and healthy environmental monitoring activities in respect of ambient air, stack emmissions and effluents are being carried out regularly to ensure good work environment. Several schemes have been introduced for recycling all toxic spilages in Coal chemicals plant, so as to improve the quality of effluent and tar sludge is being recycled in coke oven batteries to prevent accumulation of waste and to also generate extra revenue.

The private sector companies like Mukand Ltd., Sunflag Iron & Steel Co. Ltd. and Mahindra Ugine Co. Ltd are among some of the Companies making efforts to keep the pollution levels within the prescribed acceptable limits.

Welfare of schedule castes/ scheduled tribes and minorities

The Public Sector Undertakings under the administrative control of the Department of Steel continued their efforts for filling up the backlog vacancies in respect of Scheduled Castes/ Scheduled Tribes/Other Backward Classes.

The Public Sector Undertakings have also continued the process of identifying and implementing programmes aimed at the upliftment of these communities in the peripheral areas around their area of operation.

Implementation of official language policy

The progressive use of Hindi in the Department, its attached office and public sector undertakings has been widely encouraged. PSUs are given incentives by awarding Chal Vaijayanti (Running Shield); Shields and Trophies. Under an incentive scheme cash prizes of Rs.15,000/-, Rs.10,000/- and Rs.7,500/- are awarded to the writers of original books in Hindi on steel and its allied subject.

A Hindi fortnight was organised in the Department from 1 "Sept., 1998 to 15th Sept., 1998. Various competitions were held during this period and winner were awarded cash prizes. The Honourable Steel Minister made an appeal to all the officers and staff of the Deptt., attached office and PSUs to further increase the use of Hindi in their official work.

2

Highlights

Mineral law and policy

The Ministry of Steel and Mines, Department of Mines, continued the ongoing process of consolidating the steps taken in the wake of enunciation of the National Mineral Policy, 1993.

These policy changes have attracted many multinational companies for investment in mineral exploration and mining. Forty three proposals for prospecting over large areas in pursuance of the October, 1996 guidelines covering an area of about 60,000 sq. kms. in the States of Rajasthan, Gujarat, Maharashtra, Uttar Pradesh and Bihar have so far been cleared. Out of these, 20 Prospecting Licences involving an area of about 30,000 sq. kms. in the States of Rajasthan, Gujarat, Maharashtra and Bihar have been granted during the first nine months of 1998-99. Prospecting Licences have been granted in favour of Indian subsidiaries of well-known international mining companies like BHP Mineral of Australia, Meridien Peak Resources of Canada, Metdist of UK, Phelps Dodge Corporation of USA and Rio Tinto of UK. Aerial prospecting has already been completed over an area of more than 18,000 sq. kms. in Rajasthan and the licencees are very upbeat about the anomalies found so far. Further, a Secretary-level Inter-Ministerial Committee has been set up to facilitate removal of bottlenecks pertaining to grant of security clearance for undertaking aerial exploration, import of aircraft and its inspection etc. and the Department of Mines has been designated as the nodal agency. It is expected that the tempo will pick up during the next financial year.

The Foreign Investment Promotion Board (FIPB) has so far cleared 51 proposals involving Foreign Direct Investment (FDI) of about Rs. 3158 crores in the mining sector. Out of these, 12 proposals with FDI amounting to Rs. 474 crores were cleared in the first nine months of 1998-99.

To further operationalise the policy initiatives, the Government is considering greater delegation of powers to the State Governments and major procedural simplification by amending the Mines & Minerals (Regulation and Development) Act, 1957.

A National Committee under the Chairmanship of Secretary (Mines), co-chaired by Secretary, Ministry of Environment and Forests was constituted on 15.4.1998 to monitor and review environmental aspects of mining activities.

Mineral development

The total value of mineral production (excluding atomic minerals) during 1998-99 is estimated to be Rs.40,677 crores.

Public sector undertakings

In conformity with Government policy to balance the autonomy of PSUs commensurate with accountability and to set mutually acceptable targets, Memoranda of Understanding (MOU) were signed for 1998-99 with NALCO, BALCO, HZL, HCL and MECL. Greater autonomy is expected to result in quicker decision making, enhancing efficiency and increasing productivity of the

MOU signing PSUs.

National aluminium company ltd. (NALCO) made a net profit of Rs.625.43 crores (PBT) during 1997-98. The project of expansion of capacity of NALCO's Aluminium Smelter from 2,30,000 TPA to 3,45,000 TPA and that of the Captive Power Plant from 720 MW to 840 MW at a cost of Rs.2062 crores (June, 1997 price level) has been approved by the Government. The project is to be completed within 51 months from the date of Government's approval i.e. 3.2.1998. Currently, the project is under implementation by NALCO. The project of expansion of bauxite mines from 2.4 MTPY to 4.8 -MTPY and that of Alumina Refinery from 0.8 MTPY to 1.575 MTPY at a cost of Rs.1664.60 crores is also progressing as per schedule.

Bharat aluminium company ltd. (BALCO) achieved the highest ever turnover of Rs. 848.51 crores for the year 1997-98 and earned a net profit of Rs. 134.79 crores (PBT) in 1997-98. The project of setting up of new Cold Rolling Mill at a cost of Rs. 157.50 crores is under implementation by the Company.

Hindustan zinc ltd. (HZL) had a record sales turnover of Rs.1233.74 crores and earned a profit of Rs.201.77 crores (PBT) during 1997-98 which is, the highest since the inception of the Company. Two of its major units - Rampura-Agucha Lead Zinc Mine and Debari Zinc Smelter have been accredited with ISO 9002 Quality Management Certification.

Granite development council

The Granite Development Council was reconstituted vide Resolution dated 24.4.1998 for the development of granite industry and export of granite from the country. An Expert Committee was also constituted vide Resolution dated 27.4.1998, which will work under the overall guidance and supervision of the Granite Development

Council for examination of rates of royalty and dead rent fixed by different States and to suggest some broad uniformity in these rates for the overall development of the granite industry.

The geological survey of India

Surveys: A total, of 430 sq.km. was covered by systematic mapping in the North Eastern Region. Out of the country's total mappable area of 3.146 million sq.km., about 3.083 million sq. km. i.e. 98% (approx.) has so far been covered by systematic geological mapping.

Mineral investigations: In connection with mineral investigations, 2893.76 sq.km. of large scale mapping, 48.53 sq.km. detailed mapping and 53319.46 m. of drilling were done.

Additional reserves/resources established in the course of mineral exploration during the year are as follows:

- 1373 million tonnes of coal in Talcher, Godavari valley, Tattapani-Ramkola, Mand-Raigarh, Hasdo-Arand, Rajmahal and Raniganj coal fields.
- 1.64 trillion cu.ft. of Coal Bed Methane (CBM) in Birbhum and eastern part of North Karanpura coal field.
- 0.63 million tonnes of gold ore with an average grade of 3.54 g/t Au in Chikkanahalli South Block, Karnataka.
- 0.70 million tonnes of gold ore with 7.20 g/t Au in Dona East Block, Andhra Pradesh.
- 0.125 million tonnes of gold ore with 2.6 g/t of gold in Marupar-Kitari area, Maharashtra.
- 0.85 million tonnes of ore with 2.25% Pb+Zn (lead+zinc) in South Sindesar Ridge of Dariba-Bethumni belt, Rajasthan.

- 1.14 million tonnes of ore with 3.82% Pb+Zn in Latio-Ka-Khera East Block of Dariba-Bethumni belt, Rajasthan.
- 0.484 million tonnes of molybdenum ore with an average grade of 0.11 % Mo in Marudipatti Central block, Tamil Nadu.
- Re-categorised reserve of 884 million tonnes of SMS Grade and Cement Grade Limestone in Litang river valley block, Meghalaya.
- Potential zones of basemetal mineralisation have been delineated in Banskhapa-Pipariya block, Betul district, M.P.
- Significant gold values have also been reported from Puttumala West block and Kottathara block (7.6 ppm. average grade gold) in Kerala, Sonadehi prospect (upto 11.76 ppm gold) Bastar district, M.P.
- Several kimberlite pipes have been identified in Andhra Pradesh and Karnataka. These include three kimberlite bodies in Kalyandurg area of Anantapur district, Andhra Pradesh, one in Muligiripalle, and one in Yagapur in Karnataka. It may be mentioned here that this is the first report of kimberlite emplacement within the Closepet Granite. One of the three kimberlite bodies at Kalyandurg has yielded one microdiamond. Processing of a total of 972 tonnes of material from Anumpalle, Dibbasanipalle and Golapalle Kimberlite bodies has produced 24 diamonds weighing 3.58 ct. 2 diamonds weighing 2.15 ct. and 15 diamonds weighing 2.28 ct.
- A high platinum rich breccia zone (5.95 pprn to 7.15 ppm Pt.) has been identified in the southern extension of the already known PGM-mineralised zone of Boula-Nausahi area, Orissa.

- High incidence of Cesium and Lithium have been reported from Beku Pegmatite body in Chhotanagpur Gneissic Complex in West Bengal.
- A 10 m. wide band of high grade limestone extending over 20 km. from Gempalle to Lingala, in Cuddalore district, Andhra Pradesh, has been reported.

Expedition to antarctica : An area of about 1000 sq.km. was geologically mapped on 1:50,000 scale in the eastern part of Muhling-Hoffmanfjella. GSI is participating in the ongoing XVIIIth Expedition to Antarctica.

International co-operation

The first meeting of the Indo-South African Working Group on Geology and Mineral Resources, set up in pursuance of the Agreement on Co-operation in the fields of Geology and Mineral Resources signed between the two countries was held in South Africa from the 13th to the 19th August, 1998. At the end of the Working Group meeting, a Protocol was signed in Cape Town on the 18th August, 1998.

The 12th meeting of the Indo-French Working Group on Mineral Exploration and Development was held in Paris on the 7th and 8th October, 1998. The meeting prioritised five new projects amounting to FF 48.95 million (Rs.35.77 crores) and recommended for inclusion under the Indo-French Financial Protocol. The cooperation with BRGM, France, has so far resulted in flow of FF 137.88 million (Rs.100 crores approx.) assistance to upgrade equipment and skills in the GSI, IBM, MECL and some State Geological Departments.

The 5th meeting of the Indo-Russian Working Group on Ferrous and Non-Ferrous Metallurgy was held in Moscow on the 24th and 25th November, 1998. The Russians have offered technology transfers, including upgradation of old Soviet Hot Rolling Mill and Aluminum Smelter of BALCO in Madhya Pradesh.

The first 'Pride of India' Exhibition was held in Vietnam from the 14th to the 17th January, 1998. HZL and NALCO had set up stalls in the exhibition which were widely appreciated. Following the success of the first exhibition, the 2nd 'Pride of India' Exhibition was held in Hanoi from the 23rd to 26th October, 1998. The prospects of the Pac Lang Joint Venture gold project between HZL, La-Source, France and Vietnam Minerals Corporation was discussed with the Vietnamese authority.

Science & technology

The entire demand of nickel in India, which is presently around 25,000 MT, is met through imports. In order to produce this important metal in the country, technology has been developed through a collaborative project between HZL and CSIR. A Technology Proving Plant (TPP) at an estimated cost of Rs.10 crores is being set up at Regional Research Laboratory, Bhubaneswar The cost of TPP is being equally shared by HZL and CSIR. The foundation stone was laid by the Minister of Steel & Mines on 7.9.1998. If the TPP is successful, commercial production of nickel through chromite overburden, which is available in plenty, will be undertaken.

National mineral awards

The National Mineral Awards for 1997 were presented by the Minister for Steel & Mines at a function held on 24.12.1998 in New Delhi. Twelve Awards carrying a cash prize of Rs.50,000/- each were made to outstanding scientists/technologists in recognition of their meritorious contribution in their respective fields. The 'Award of Excellence' carrying a cash prize of Rs.1,00,000/- was conferred on Prof. K.S. Valdiya of the Jawaharlal Nehru Centre for Advanced Scientific Research, Bangalore, for his sustained and significant contributions in the field of geosciences.

Other events

The Department of Mines including its Public Sector Undertakings (PSUs) and Subordinate offices participated in the 5th International Mining and Machinery Exhibition (IMME'98) organized by the Confederation of Indian Industry (CII) at Pragati Maidan, New Delhi from the 26th to the 29th October, 1998.

A 'Mega Event' was organized by the Department of Mines to celebrate the 50th year of India's Independence at Nagpur from the 6th to 8th August, 1998. The Indian Bureau of Mines, a subordinate office of this Department, also celebrated its Golden Jubilee.

3

Iron and Steel Industry

Steel is crucial to the development of any modern economy and is considered to be the backbone of the human civilisation. The level of per capita consumption of steel is treated as one of the important indicators of socio-economic development and living standard of the people in any country. It is a product of a large and technologically complex industry having strong forward and backward linkages in terms of material flow and income generation. All major industrial economies are characterised by the existence of a strong steel industry and the growth of many of these economies has been largely shaped by the strength of their steel industries in their initial stages of development.

Historical perspective

The finished steel production in India has grown from a mere 1.1 million tonnes in 1951 to 23.372 million tonnes in 1997-98. During the first two decades of planned economic development, i.e. 1950-60 and 1960-70 the average annual growth rate of steel production exceeded 8%. However, this growth rate could not be maintained in the decades to follow. During 1970-80, the growth rate in steel production came down to 5.7% per annum and picked up marginally to 6.4% per annum during 1980-90. Though India started steel production in 1911, steel exports from India began only in 1964. Exports in the first five years were mainly due to recession in the domestic iron and steel market. Once domestic demand revived, exports declined. India once again started exporting steel only in 1975 touching a figure of 1 million tonne of pig iron export and 1.4 million tonnes of steel export in 1976-77. Thereafter, exports again fell rapidly to meet rising domestic demand.

Only after liberalisation of the steel sector the exports of iron and steel have once again started increasing. Though the country's production of iron and steel is sufficient to meet the domestic demand, however, some quantity of steel is always needed to be imported especially those grades and qualities which are required in small quantities, and therefore do not justify setting up of production capacities.

The progress of the steel industry has a critical influence on the pace of India's development and as such great importance is attached to capacity expansion in line with expected demand at cost and prices, which make Indian steel internationally competitive. The new economic policies being pursued by the Government have opened up new opportunities for the expansion of the steel industry. With a view to accelerating the growth of the steel sector, the Government has initiated a number of policy measures since 1991.

Liberalisation of the Indian steel sector

The important policy measures which have been taken for growth and development of the Indian Iron & Steel Sector are as under :

In the new industrial policy announced in July, 1991 Iron and Steel Industry, among others, was removed from the list of industries reserved for the public sector and also exempted from the provisions of compulsory licensing under the Industries (Development and Regulation) Act, 1951.

With effect from 24.5.92 iron and steel industry was included in the fist of 'high priority' industries for automatic approval for foreign equity investment upto 51% (now 74%). Price and distribution of steel were deregulated from January, 1992. At the same time, it was ensured that priority continued to be accorded for meeting the requirements of small scale industries, exporters of engineering goods and North Eastern Region, besides strategic sectors such as Defence and Railways.

The import regime for iron and steel has undergone major liberalisation moving gradually from a controlled import by way of import licensing, foreign exchange release, canalisation and high import tariffs to total freeing of iron and steel imports from licencing, canalisation and lowering of import duty levels. Export of iron and steel items was also freely allowed.

Import duty on capital goods was reduced from 55% to 25%. Duties on raw materials for steel production were reduced. These measures reduced the capital costs and production costs of steel plants.

Freight equalisation scheme was withdrawn in January '92, removing freight disadvantage to states located near steel plants. At the same time, it was ensured that far-flung areas and distant states were protected by stipulating that beyond the freight ceiling distance, the main producers would continue to bear the freight charges.

Levy on account of Steel Development Fund was discontinued from April'94 providing greater flexibility to main producers to respond to market forces.

Current global scenario

After recording a growth rate of 3.2 in 1996 over the previous year crude steel production world wide went up by over 6% in the first half of 1997 over the corresponding period of the previous year. However, during the second half of 1997 and in the first half of 1998, production of steel worldwide has shown signs of slowing down. In fact, the markets in EU, USA and Japan continued to remain depressed through out 1997 in 1998 as a result of financial crisis gripping several world economies, especially in CIS and South East Asian nations.

The developing countries, in particular those in South East Asia continue to remain the focus of attention in so far as the dynamics of the steel industry for India is concerned. Till these markets improve, India will continue to face problems in exporting iron and steel. On the pricing front, with the emergence of Latin America, South Korea, Taiwan, India and lately the CIS as significant exporters, the role of European and Japanese producers as major exporters and consequently as price makers has been reduced making the market much more competitive.

It is in this global context that the steel industry countries like India will have to cast their future role.

Growth of the Indian steel sector after liberalisation

Today, India is the 10th largest steel producing country in the world. This sector represents around Rs. 90,000 crores of capital and directly provides employment to over 5 lakh of people. The Indian steel sector was the first core sector to be completely freed from the licencing regime and the pricing and distribution controls.

This was done primarily because of the inherent strengths and capabilities demonstrated by the Indian iron and steel industry. During 1996-97, finished steel production shot up to a record 22.72 million tonnes with a growth rate of 6.2% while in 1997-98 the finished steel production increased to 23.37 million tonnes, which was 2.8% more than the previous year. The growth rate has drastically decreased in the last 2 years, being only 6.2% in 1996-97 and 2.8% in 1997-98, as compared to 17.24% in 1994-95 and 20% in 1995-96.

This sharp fall in the growth rate of steel production has been brought about by several factors which inter alia, include, general slow down in the industrial production and construction activities in the country coupled with lack of growth in major steel consuming sectors. The total production of finished steel and the share of main and secondary producers during 90's and upto the present has been as follows:

Year	Main producers	Secondary Producers	Total
1991-92	7.96 (55%)	6.37 (45%)	14.33
1992-93	8.41 (55%)	6.79 (45%)	15.20
1993-94	8.77 (57.6%)	6.43 (42.4%)	15.20
1994-95	9.57 (53.8%)	8.25 (46.2%)	17.82
1995-96	10.59 (49.5%)	10.81 (50.5%)	21.40
1996-97	10.54 (46.4%)	12.18 (53.6%)	22.72
1997-98	10.44 (44.6%)	12.93 (55.4%)	23.37

After delicensing of iron and steel industry and as a result of the steps taken for creation of additional capacity in the private sector, as on 1.6.98, All India Financial Institutions have cleared 19 projects involving an annual capacity of about 13 million tonnes of saleable steel at an investment of Rs.25,000 crores.

Out of these, 6 projects involving about Rs.6070 crores have already been commissioned with an annual capacity of 3.54 million tonnes. Other projects are at various stages of implementation. Thus it will be seen that in the years to come, the percentage production of the private sector will be much larger than production of the public sector in the steel industry.

Pig Iron

Along with the production of steel, the production of pig iron in the country during the period 1991-92 to the present has also increased. The details are as under :

Year	Main Producers	Secondary Producers	Total
1991-92	1.485	0.102	1.587
1992-93	1.679	0.165	1.844
1993-94	1.977	0.237	2.250
1994-95	2.005	0.780	2.785
1995-96	1.735	1.060	2.795
1996-97	1.733	1.557	3.290
1997-98	1.76	1.687	3.393
(April-Dec.)	1.072	1.086	2.158

During the last 2 years alone, sponge iron production went up by over 1. 1 million tonne. Today, India is the second largest producer of sponge iron in the world. The production of sponge iron in the country has also resulted in providing an alternative feed material to steel melting scrap which was hitherto imported in large quantities by the Electric Arc Furnace Unit and the Induction Furnace Unit. This has resulted in considerable saving in foreign exchange.

Sponge Iron

During the early 90s, sponge iron industry had been specially promoted so as to provide an alternative to steel melting scrap which was increasingly becoming scarce. The production of sponge iron (Direct Reduced Iron - DRI) during the period 1991-92 to the present was as under:

(Quantity in million tonnes)

Year	Production	%Increase
1991-92	1.31	-
1992-93	1.44	9.9
1993-94	2.40	66.7
1994-95	3.39	41.3
1995-96	4.40	29.8
1996-97	5.01	13.8
1997-98	5.35	6.78
(April-Dec.)	3.85	-

Apparent consumption of steel

The long term projections of steel demand, which formed the basis of capacity planning during Second and Third Five Year Plans were based on an optimistic rise in per capita consumption of steel and high absorption of steel in the economy. This optimism was based on the growth rates of different sectors, structural changes in the economy and import substitution. The finished steel consumption which was only 18.66 Million Tonnes in 1994-95 has increased to 22.63 million tonnes in 1997-98.

India's per capita crude steel consumption as per the figures available for 1997, was only 22 Kg, which is far below the level of other developed and developing countries -395 kg., 289 kg. and 84 kg. in USA, the EU (15) and China. The World average was around 126 Kg. in 1997. With the ongoing economic liberalisation resulting in faster economic growth, the steel consumption is expected to increase rapidly.

Apparent consumption of steel is arrived at by subtracting export of steel from the total of domestic production and import of steel in the country. Change in stock is also adjusted in arriving at the consumption figures. It is also treated as the actual domestic demand of steel in the country. The year-wise apparent consumption of finished steel since 1990-91 is given in the table below:

Table-II : I

(In Million Tonnes)

Year	ApparentConsumption
1990-91	14.37
1991-92	14.83 (3.2%)
1993-94	15.32 (1.2%)
1994-95	18.66 (21.8%)
1995-96	21.65 (16.0%)
1996-97	22.13 (2.27%)
1997-98	22.63 (2.28%)

The apparent consumption of steel did not show much increase in 1997-98 mainly due to slowdown being faced by some of the steel using industries like automobile and engineering industries and construction. With the revival of the demand for automobile and engineering goods and general improvement in the economy, it is expected that consumption of steel will increase further.

Long term demand availability projections of finished steel

In order to have a long term perspective and planning, a Working Group for IXth Five Year Plan was constituted for iron and steel sector under the aegis of Planning Commission. The Working Group deliberated upon all aspects including supply-demand projections for finished steel during the terminal years of VIIIth and IXth Five Year Plans i.e. 1996-97 and 2001-02, taking a GDP growth rate of 5% during the VIIIth Plan and 6% thereafter and a GDP elasticity of demand for steel of 1.33. The Working Group also suggested various strategies for an integrated and harmonious growth of the steel sector during IXth Plan period and thereafter.

The Ministry of Steel (9th Plan Working Group) has estimated that the demand for finished steel (including demand for exports) in 2001-02 would touch 38.68 million tonnes. The domestic availability of finished steel from all sources for 1997-98 was about 23.37 million tonnes. It is expected that by 2001-02, it would be 38.01 million tonnes. The projected availability is almost adequate to meet the domestic demand and also export potential of 6 million tonnes as identified by the Working Group during 9th Five Year Plan period. The installed capacity is expected to reach 43.606 million tonnes by the end of the Ninth Five Year Plan. Similarly, by 2006-07 the demand for finished steel is estimated to be of the order of 48.80 million tonnes, whereas production in the country would be 57.80 million tonnes, providing adequate surplus for meeting the projected export potential of 9 million tonnes.

The major public sector integrated steel plants of SAIL including TISCO and RINL, would be able to contribute about 11.449 million tonnes and 2.41 million tonnes respectively. With TISCO's contribution of 3.1 million tonnes of finished steel, the integrated steel plants are expected to produce 16.959 million tonnes.

The balance 21,053 million tonnes would be from secondary steel sector during 2001-02. In other words, the Secondary Sector is expected to contribute about 55.4 percent of the availability of finished steel in the country.

The Working Group has identified the following pattern of the investment during the Ninth Five Year Plan:

Table-II: 2

(in crore)

Area	Public Sector	Private Sector	Total
Steel	16, 202.00	31, 658.00	47,860.00
Sponge Iron	000.00	635.00	635.00
Pig Iron	0.00	200.00	200.00
Raw Material and Others	3,479.00	0.00	3,479.00

It will be seen that out of total estimation of investment of Rs.52,174.00 crore in iron and steel sector during IXth Plan period made by the Working Group, public sector's contribution was expected to account for about 38% and the balance 62% of the investment supposed to be coming from the private sector. But subsequently, the Planning Commission undertook a detailed and in-depth exercise to determine the exact investment, which the Public Sector Undertakings in the Steel Sector would be expected to make during the Plan period. The Planning Commission has finally approved a Plan Outlay Rs.19,197.88 crore for PSUs for IXth Five Year Plan. The total approved outlay of Rs.19,197.88 crore for IXth Five Year Plan for public sector undertakings includes a Budgetary Support of only Rs.90.00 crore, which constitutes only 0.47%. The remaining investment proposed to be made by PSUs will be met from their internal accruals and extra budgetary resources.

In so far as private sector is concerned, as mentioned in para 5.4 earlier, the All India Financial Institutions have cleared 19 medium/large projects involving an annual capacity of approximately 13 million tonnes of saleable steel and investment of over Rs.25,000 crore.

Ministry of Steel has formulated a well-knit scheme in consultation with Planning Commission for self-reliant and healthy growth of the steel sector keeping in view all gamuts of growth perspective for this sector. This includes maintaining continuous growth coupled with projected investments both in public and private sectors as well as investment for raising technological and managerial skills, quick decision making for product planning, man-power deployment, etc.

Distribution of iron and steel

As a part of the economic liberalisation process, the Government of India, on 16th January, 1992, abolished the price regulation of the Joint Plant Committee (JPC) on iron and steel, which had been in existence since 1964. However, the requirements of Defence, Railways, Small Scale Industries Sector, exporters of engineering goods and the North Eastern Region continue to be met on priority at prices that are announced by the producers from time to time.

The Development Commissioner for Iron & Steel continues to make allocations of pig iron to the designated consumers and the main producers supply the material on the basis of such allocation. To meet the requirements of steel of Small Scale Industries, allocations are made by the Development Commissioner for Iron & Steel. This is in addition to the purchases made by Small Scale Units, which draw their materials directly from the main producers. The Development Commissioner also continues to issue Release Orders for supplies to exporters of engineering goods and make annual supply plans for the North Eastern Region. The requirements of Defence and Railways are met by the main producers directly on priority in accordance with the past procedures.

Considering the special problems in meeting the requirements of consumers in the North-Eastern Region, special efforts are made to ensure adequate and timely supplies to that region.

Pricing of iron & steel

The pricing mechanism of the Joint Plant Committee (JPC) operating from 1964 was abolished with effect from 16th January, 1992. Producers are now free to determine and announce their prices, which are now governed by market forces of demand and supply.

After deregulation, the main producers, i.e., Steel Authority of India Limited, Rashtriya Ispat Nigam Ltd. and TISCO are charging either the actual freight upto stockyard or freight element as it existed prior to deregulation (now Rs.1710/- per tonne in case of steel and Rs.1165/- per tonne in case of pig iron), whichever is lower. This has ensured that far flung areas and distant States are protected by stipulating that the main producers shall charge either actual freight or freight element existing prior to withdrawal of the scheme, whichever is less.

Import and export of iron and steel

The general policy and procedures for export and import of iron and steel, ferro alloys and ferro scrap are at present decided by the Ministry of Commerce in consultation with Ministry of Steel.

With the liberalisation of India's trade policy and commencement of the export-import policy for 5 years (from 1.4.1997 to 31.3.2002), the policy for import and export of iron and steel materials has undergone sweeping changes. Import of A items of iron and steel is freely allowed.

The value-based advanced licence and the old pass-book scheme has been replaced by a new scheme-Duty Entitlement Pass-Book (DEPB) scheme -which combines the positive features of both the schemes besides being easy to administer and more transparent. Under this, scheme, exporters on the basis of notified entitlement rates, will be granted due credits, which would entitle them to import goods duty free.

Exports of all items of iron and steel are also freely allowed. Exports of high grade iron ore, chrome ore and manganese ore are made through designated canalising agencies subject to the ceilings imposed by the Government, in order to conserve high grade ores for domestic consumption and production of value added materials.

Consistent efforts are being made by the Ministry of Steel/Development Commissioner for Iron and Steel to ensure adequate supplies of domestic raw materials to meet requirements of engineering exporters.

Import of steel

India had been annually importing about 10 to 15 lakh tonnes of steel. However, due to picking up of domestic demand, the import of saleable steel in 1994-95 increased to 1.93 million tonnes. The increase in import was mainly in hot rolled coils, cold rolled coils and semis. Import of saleable steel during 1997-98 was about 1.81 million tonnes which was about 1.5% higher than import in 1996-97.

Export by iron and steel sector

It may be mentioned at the outset that India has already registered its presence in the global market in the recent years. While India started steel production in the year 1911, steel exports from India started only in 1964. However, steel exports have been sporadic in the initial years. From 1964 to 1968 India exported a large quantity of steel mainly due to recession in the domestic iron and

Table-II Export of Steel and Pig and Steel

(*Quality in lakh tonnes*) Value in Rs. crore

Year	Saleable Steel		Pig Iron		Sponge Iron		Total Iron&Steel	
	Qty	Value	Qty.	Value	Qty.	Value	Qty.	Value
1992-93	8.94	7.02	0.16	6	2.00	80	11.10	788
1993-94	16.01	1417	6.20	261	7.00	300	29.21	1978
1994-95	13.19	1238	4.67	200	6.66	280	24.52	1718
1995-96	15.02	20.39	4.06	192	3.80	165	27.08	2396
1997-98	18.78	2343	7.84	404	3.74	190	30.36	2937

steel market. Subsequently, exports declined with revival of domestic demand. India once again started exporting steel from 1975, touching a record export of steel in 1976-77. In the year 1976-77. India exported 1 million tonne of pig iron and 1.4 million tonnes of steel. Thereafter, exports again declined only to pick up in 1991-92, when main producers exported 3.87 lakh tonnes valued at Rs. 283 crore.

As a result of various policy measures taken up by the Government like liberalisation of import-export policy, introduction of flexibility in the advance licensing scheme and convertibility of rupee on the capital account. The export of Iron and Steel (including Sponge Iron) showed a quantum jump to 2.92 million tonnes valued at Rs. 1978 crore in 1993-94. In 1995-96, the export was of the order of 2.79 million tonnes valued at Rs. 2,275 crore. The export of Iron & Steel during 1996-97 was 2.71 million tonnes valued at Rs.2,396 crore. During 1997-98, the export of iron and steel was a record 3.04 million tonnes valued at Rs. 2,937 crores.

Earlier, exports consisted mainly of plates, structurals, bars and rods, whereas now apart from semis, hot rolled coils, cold rolled coils, colour coated sheets, GP/GC sheets, pig iron and sponge iron are also being exported. In future, it is expected that the exports of more value added items will increase.

Steel exporters forum

The Department of Steel has set up a Steel Exporters Forum in February 1998 with a view to fulfil the long felt need of the producers and exporters from the iron and steel sector and also to resolve issues, problems and bottlenecks faced by them in exports. The Chairman of the Forum is the Development Commissioner for Iron and Steel and all major steel producers/ associations are its members. Representatives of the Ministries of Finance,

Railways and Surface Transport are also its members in addition to the Department of Steel.

Indian steel is exported to China, Japan, USA, Korea, Taiwan, Indonesia, Thailand, Malaysia, Italy, U.K., Germany, Canada, Spain, Australia, etc.

The IXth Plan Working Group for Iron and Steel has estimated that India will have an export potential of 6 million tonnes of steel by 2001-02 and 9 million tonnes by 2006-07. The above projection for export has been made keeping in view the need for projecting export as a distinct market, which need to be developed, of course, after meeting the domestic requirements.

Functions of the office of development commissioner for iron & steel

The Office of Development Commissioner for Iron and Steel (DCI&S) through its Regional Offices continued to perform its advisory, developmental and regulatory functions during the year.

With the deregulation of distribution and pricing of iron and steel, the major functions of the Development Commissioner for Iron and Steel are as follows :

- Collection, processing and dissemination of basic information relating to the Iron and Steel industry and to act as the data bank of the Department of Steel
- Monitoring of regional price and supply trends and suggesting to the Department remedial measures for correcting the imbalances, if any.
- Monitoring of import and export of iron and steel materials.
- Advice on matters relating to import and export policies of iron and steel.

- Management of distribution of iron and steel materials to the designated priority sectors such as, Defence, Railways, State Small Industries Corporations, Engineering Goods Exporters and the North Eastern States,
- Allocation of materials to the State Small Scale Industry Corporations.
- Allocation of materials to remote areas like North Eastern States
- Assistance to Engineering Goods Export Units through priority allocations and monitoring thereof.
- Survey of various segments of Steel Industry
- Rendering assistance to the EAF Units and the secondary sector, by way of capacity assessment, assistance in procurement of indigenous/imported raw materials and import substitution measures aimed at overall development of the sector.
- Interface between the Government and different consumer groups to facilitate consumer - producer interaction.
- Co-ordination for movement of raw materials to Steel Plants
- Vigilance functions to prevent misuse of steel obtained from regulated sources.

Reasons for current slow down of the iron and steel sector

The iron and steel sector has been experiencing a slow down in the recent past.. The growth of the steel sector is dependent upon the growth of the economy in general and the growth of industrial production and infrastructure sectors in particular. The major reasons for the slow growth in the last few years include:-

Sluggish demand in the steel consuming sectors

Steel being the basic raw material for the construction industry, the capital goods and engineering goods industry, as also the auto sector and white goods sector, its growth is dependent upon the demand for steel by these segments of the industry. Since no major infrastructure or construction projects have been implemented in the last few years, demand for steel has remained low. No major projects in the oil sector, power sector, fertiliser sector where intensity of steel consumption is high, have come up in the recent past.

Overall economic slow down in the country

All major core sectors of the economy have been facing an economic slow down. These include, power, coal, cement, industry, mining and steel. The slow down phenomenon is not restricted to the steel sector alone. Only when the overall economy of the country picks up, would the steel sector also show signs of revival.

Lack of investment by Government/private sector in major infrastructure projects

Due to budgetary constraints, no major construction activity in mega projects including fertiliser, power, coal, railways etc. have been planned by the Government. Despite liberalisation of the economy and relaxation in the investment norms, private sector investment is yet to materialise in the core sectors of the economy. This has also contributed in slowing down demand for steel.

Cost escalation in the input materials for iron and steel

Power tariff, freight rates, coal prices etc. have been under the administered price regime. These rates have been frequently enhanced, thereby contributing to the rise in input costs for steel making.

Continuous reduction in import duty on iron and steel

After liberalisation import duty rates on iron and steel items have been gradually reduced over the years. This has opened up the domestic iron and steel sector to international competition. The table I below indicates the extent of changes brought about in the customs duty of some of the items of steel since 1992-93:

Continuous increase in excise duty on iron and steel

During the period 1991-92 onwards upto 1994-95, the iron arid steel materials have been constantly subjected to an increase in the excise duty rates, as is evident from the table below. Even in the year 1995-96, though there was no increase in rate of excise duty, the methodology of computation of excise duty was widened by adding to the ex-factory prices, the stockyard and distribution charges in the basic price. This resulted in increase in the prices of steel all over the country. Whereas in other sectors of the economy, drastic reduction in excise duties were announced during 1994-95 & 1995-96. In fact, the steel sector is the highest revenue earner for the country and contributes about Rs.5,000 crores by way of excise duty alone. It is high time that the burden on the consumers of steel of such a high excise duty of 15% is reduced.

Excise Duty Rates

	1992-93	1993-94	1994-95	1995-96	1996-97	1997-98 &98-99
HR Coils	11.5%	12.5%	15%	15%	15%	15%
CR Coils	11.55	15%	15%	15%	15%	15%
Plates	11.5%	12.5%	15%	15%	15%	15%

Greater competition from imports

Due to the drastic reduction in import duties on iron and steel materials along with sharp fall in international prices, the imports of finished steel even in those sectors where adequate capacity exists have shown an increasing trend.

Dumping of finished steel in the country

Taking advantage of lower tariff regime and the unrestricted import of all iron and steel materials with the liberalisation of the EXIM policy, some countries are reportedly dumping their finished steel products in India.

Adverse conditions in export markets for iron and steel

Due to economic crisis, the South East Asian countries, the traditional market for Indian iron and steel exports has dried up. Countries, which were hitherto importing steel from India, have cut down on imports to conserve scarce resources and Indian exporters have been forced to look for newer markets elsewhere in the globe. These countries particularly Indonesia, Malaysia & Korea in fact, have now become competitors to Indian exports in other global markets.

Action being taken by department of steel

The Department of Steel has been making all out efforts to help the domestic steel sector to overcome the problems faced by the steel industry at present. These include :

a) Sluggish demand in the steel consuming sectors

To boost the demand and consumption of steel, an Institute for Steel Development and Growth (INSDAG) has been set up in Calcutta with leading steel producers in the country as its members. The Development commissioner for Iron & Steel (DCI&S) has launched a National Camp= for increasing the demand for steel, in non-traditional sectors, particularly in the construction, rural and agro based industrial sector.

b) Duty on project imports

To enhance the consumption of steel in the country, the Finance Ministry has been urged to provide a level playing field to domestic steel producers for steel supply against International Competitive Bidding (ICB) under 'project imports' in the fertilizer, power, oil sectors by exempting them for excise and sales tax.

c) Reduction in power & rail tariffs

The Department of Steel has been interacting with State Governments to provide power at reduced/concessional tariffs especially to mini steel plants all over the country. Similarly, the freight rates adopted by the Railways have been rationalised after inter action with the Railway Board and freight cost on raw material transportation for steel producers is reduced.

d) Reduction in input costs

The Department of Steel has also been able to rationalise the classification of coking coal in consultation with the Coal Ministry so as to reduce the impact of royalty payable on this basic raw material. Import duties on several raw materials, such as, scrap, ships for breaking, coke, non-coking coal etc. used by the steel industry has been reduced steadily over the past 4-5 years.

e) Import duty

In the last two Budgets, import dudes on finished steel items have remained at the same levels as suggested by Department of Steel.

Excise duty

The Finance Ministry was requested not to resort to further increase in Excise Duties on iron and steel materials, in the last few budgets. On the other hand, a case has been made to reduce the excise duty levels on all finished steel items, especially long products (which are consumed by the construction sector) by at least 10%, as the construction sector cannot avail of MODVAT benefit.

To check the increasing trend of cheap imports in certain categories of flat products especially from CIS and South East Asian countries, the Department of Steel has urged the Commerce Ministry and the Finance Ministry to strengthen anti dumping mechanism so that fast decision on dumping can be taken.

h) Working Group

Recently, in response to the strong plea made by the Minister for Steel, the Finance Minister had set up a Working Group headed by Secretary (Banking) to study the problems faced by the steel industry and give suitable recommendations. The Working Group has suggested various measures for implementation by Finance and Commerce Ministries, AD India Financial Institutions and the steel producers. These measures are in various stages of examination/implementation.

Future prospects

With the onset of liberalisation, the steel industry has now to gear-up, not only to domestic competition, but also to global competition in terms of product range, quality and price. The growth of the steel sector is intricately linked with the growth of the Indian economy and especially the growth of the steel consuming sectors. India has become self-sufficient in iron and steel materials in the last 3-4 years. Exports are rising and imports are falling. Production and production capacities are increasing. This position needs to be further consolidated and issues affecting production and consumption need to be resolved on a continuous basis. At the same time, productivity of our steel plants must be maintained at levels close to international standards. The Ministry of Steel continues to play an active and major role in helping the steel industry to overcome bottlenecks in the growth of this sector. With these efforts, the IXth Plan projection for finished steel of 32 million tonnes for domestic consumption and 6 million tonnes of export can be achieved, as also the projections for availability of 3.75 million tonnes of pig iron and 6.18 million tonnes of sponge iron.

India is already recognized as a global player in the steel industry and this sector is poised to play a key role in the international steel scenario by the turn of the century.

4

Role and Organisation of the Department of Mines

Main functions

The Department of Mines is responsible for survey and exploration of all minerals, other than natural gas, petroleum and atomic minerals; for mining and metallurgy of non-ferrous metals like aluminium, copper, zinc, lead, gold, nickel etc. and for administration of the Mines and Minerals (Regulation and Development) Act, 1957 in respect of all mines and minerals other than coal, natural gas, petroleum and atomic minerals. A list of subjects allocated to the Department of Mines, subordinate offices, public sector undertakings and research institutions under the administrative control of the Department of Mines is given at Table I & 11.

Organisational structure

Headed by the Secretary, the Department of Mines comprises an Additional Secretary, an Additional Secretary and Financial Adviser, who is common for the Department of Steel and Department of Mines, two Joint Secretaries, one Adviser (S&T), five Directors, three Deputy Secretaries, one Senior Principal Private Secretary, five Under Secretaries, one Deputy Director (Official Language), one Principal Private Secretary, fifteen Section Officers, seven Private Secretaries, one

Junior Scientific Officer and one Assistant Director (Official Language). Besides this, the Department has a technical wing comprising one Industrial Adviser, one Additional Industrial Adviser, two Development Officers and two Additional Development Officers. The total number of sanctioned posts for the Secretariat of the Department of Mines is 51 Gazetted and 198 Non-Gazetted posts. In addition, there is a Chief Controller of Accounts assisted by a Pay and Accounts Officer and 35 Non-Gazetted staff in the Pay & Accounts Office.

List of subjects allocated to the department of mines

(i) Legislation for regulation of mines and development of minerals within the territory of India, including mines and minerals underlying the ocean within the territorial waters or the continental shelf, or the Exclusive Economic Zone and other Maritime Zones of India as may be specified from time to time by or under any law made by the Parliament.

(ii) Regulation of mines and development of minerals other than coal, lignite and sand for stowing and any mineral declared as prescribed substances for the purposes of the Atomic Energy Act, 1962 (33 of 1962) under the control of the Union as declared by law, including questions concerning regulation and development of minerals in various states and the matter connected therewith or incidental thereto.

All other metals and minerals not specifically allotted to any other Ministry/Department such as aluminium, zinc, copper, gold, diamond, lead and nickel.

Planning, development and control of and assistance to all industries dealt with by the Department.

Subordinate offices

There are three Subordinate Offices under the

Department of Mines, namely :-

(1) Geological Survey of India (HQ, Calcutta)
(2) Indian Bureau of Mines (HQ, Nagpur)
(3) Controller of Mining Leases (HQ, Nagpur)

Public sector undertakings

There are six PSUs and one Joint Venture Company under the Department of Mines, namely :-

(1) National Aluminium Company Ltd. (NALCO), Bhubaneswar;
(2) Bharat Aluminium Company Ltd. (BALCO), New Delhi;
(3) Hindustan Zinc Ltd. (HZL), Udaipur;
(4) Hindustan Copper Ltd. (HCL), Calcutta;
(5) Mineral Exploration Corporation Ltd. (MECL), Nagpur;
(6) Bharat Gold Mines Ltd. (BGML), Kolar Gold Fields (Karnataka);
(7) Sikkim Mining Corporation (a company jointly owned by the Government of Sikkim and the Central Government).

Research institutions

There are three Research Institutions under the Department of Mines, namely:-

(1) Jawaharlal Nehru Aluminium Research Development and Design Centre, Nagpur.
(2) National Institute of Rock Mechanics, Kolar.
(3) National Institute of Miners' Health, Kolar.

Organisations under department of mines

Survey and exploration

Geological survey of India:

Regional exploration, geological mapping, surveys on land, sea and airborne surveys and priority assignments to GSI.

Mineral exploration corporation ltd:

MECL is responsible for detailed exploration of various minerals/ores by drilling and exploratory mining and proving reserves for their eventual exploitation.

Regulation and conservation

Indian bureau of mines:

Engaged in promoting, conservation and development of mineral resources of the country.

Controller of mining leases:

The Officer deals with the work relating to modification of all such mining leases which have been granted before 1972 i.e. the date when the provisions/amendments to the MM (R&D) Act, 1957 for the purpose were made.

(The State Governments have also framed Minor Mineral Concession Rules for regulation and development of minor minerals).

Minig and processing

Bharat aluminium company ltd.:

Incorporated on 27th November, 1965 with an integrated Alumina/ Aluminium Complex at Korba in Madhya Pradesh.

Bharat gold mines ltd.:

Incorporated on 22nd March, 1972 to own and manage the mines at Kolar Gold Fields (Karnataka) w.e.f. 1.4.1972.

Hindustan zinc ltd.:

Incorporated on 10th January, 1966 after the Govt. of India took over erstwhile Metal Corporation of India to own, manage and develop the mineral and smelting capacities for the strategic zinc and lead metals in the country.

Hindustan copper ltd. :

Incorporated in November, 1967, it is presently the sole indigenous producer of primary copper in the country.

National aluminium, company ltd. :

Incorporated on 7th January, 1981 to implement the BauxiteAlumina-Aluminium Project in Orissa.

Sikkim mining corporation (in which central Government has 49% equity participation):

It produces polymetallic ore which is treated in the concentrator plant producing copper, lead and zinc concentrates.

5

Raw Materials

Iron Ore

As per the Survey conducted by the Indian Bureau of Mines (IBM) in April, 1995. India had 10,053 Million tonnes of Recoverable reserves of Hearnatites and 3,408 Million Tonnes of Magnetite. While Zone 'A' comprising of Bihar & Orissa is the largest Heamatite Ore bearing Zone in the Country with reserves of 5,951 Million Tonnes consisting mainly of Medium Grade & Low Grade Ore (Iron content 65% and below), Madhya Pradesh has the largest quantity of High Grade Ore reserves (Iron content greater than 65%) in the country at 570 Million Tonnes. Karnataka has the highest reserves of Magnetite at 2,784 Million tonnes followed by Andhra Pradesh and Goa.

Production

Production of iron ore (including concentrates) during the year 1997-98 was 73.45 million tonnes as against 68.17 million tonnes in the previous year. State-Wise production figures indicate that Madhya Pradesh would continue to be the leading iron ore producing State accounting for 26% of the total production during the year, followed by Karnataka with 22%, Goa 19%, Orissa 17% and Bihar 16%. The remaining production was from Andhra Pradesh and Maharashtra.

Despatches

Despatches of iron ore (including concentrates) for 1997-98 were 71.41 million tonnes. The despatches of iron ore for internal consumption and exports would be 40.27 million tonnes and 31.14 million tonnes respectively.

Iron Ore Exports

The exports during the year 1997-98 were at 35.26 (Prov.) million tonnes as against 29.65 (Prov.) million tonnes in 1996-97.

Manganese Ore

As per the latest inventory the recoverable reserves of manganese ore are estimated at 176 million tonnes. The main reserves found in India are of blast furnace grade. The reserves of ferro manganese grade are very limited i.e. 12% of the total reserves only.

Production

Production of manganese ore during 1997-98 was 1.60 million tonnes as against 1.81 million tonnes in 1996-97. Orissa, Madhya Pradesh, Maharastra and Karnataka were be the principal producing state accounting for 34%, 22%, 20% and 17% respectively in the total production of manganese ore in 1997-98.

Despatches

Despatches of manganese ore during 1997-98 were 1.64 million tonnes of which 1.41 million tonnes were be for internal consumption and 0.22 million tonnes for exports.

Export policy of manganese ore is decided keeping in view the need for conserving high grade ores. Alongwith this, effort is also made to replace the export of ores with export of value added items.

For the year 1997-98 the maximum ceilings of manganese ore allowed for export were as follows:

Item	Ceiling for 1997-98 (In lakh
Medium Grade Manganese Ore/blended ore containing 38% to 46% manganese and more than 0.15% Phos.	1.00
Medium Grade Manganese ore/ blended ore containing 38% to 46% manganese and more than 0.10% Phos.	0.50
Low grade manganese ore/ blended ore containing less than 38% manganese.	4.00
Manganese ore fines below 12mm in size containing less than 44% manganese.	1.50

Actual export during last two years have been as follows:

Year	Quantity (In lakh tonnes)	Value (Rs. in crores)
1996-97	4.17	58.57
1997-98	2.59	42.20

Chromite Ore

As per the latest inventory, the total recoverable reserves of chromite are estimated at 88 million tonnes. Orissa is the largest Chromite ore producing state in the country accounting historically for 96% of its total production, followed by Karnataka which produced about 4% of the total production. Small quantities are also produced in Andhra Pradesh and Manipur.

Production

Production of Chromite in 1997-98 was 15.64 lakh tonnes as against 14.56 lakh tonnes in 1996-97. Orissa continues to be the chief producing state accounting for 98% of the total production.

Despatches

Production and despatches of chromite during the year 1994-95 to 1997-98 are given below:

Year/ period ('000T)	Production Qty.	Value Rs.Crores) ('000T)	Despatches Total	For domestic consum-ption ('000T)	For Export ('000T)
1994-95	1132	252.23	1068	621	447
1995-96	1700	356.82	1597	1121	476
1996-97	1456	290.61	1224	698	526
1997-98	1564	308.67	1366	872	494

Ferro Alloys

Ferro alloys are essential additives in steel making used for imparting desired properties to steel. The product mix of ferro alloy industry mainly consists of Ferro Manganese (Fe Mn), Ferro Silicon (Fe Si.) and Ferro Chrome (Fe Cr.) - called the Bulk ferro alloys. There is another category of ferro alloys, called Noble ferro alloys, which consists of Ferro Vanadium, Ferro Titanium, Ferro Molybdenum, Ferro Niobium, Ferro Tungstun etc., whose production is negligible.

The production of ferro alloys in India started in early fifties with the industry growing manifold during these four decades. The industry is mainly concentrated in four states viz. Orissa, Maharashtra, Andhra Pradesh and Karnataka for their being rich in the basic raw materials for the production of the ferro, alloys.

Export

Keeping in view the limited reserve of Chromite ore in the country, only certain grades of ore are allowed for export. Emphasis has been laid on export of beneficiated chromite concentrates. From the year 1997-98, a five year Export policy was decided upon by Government so us to enable the exporters to establish their presence in the international market.

The maximum ceilings for export of Chromite ore for 1997-98 were as follows:

Item	Ceiling for 1997-98 (In lakh tonnes)
Low silica friable/fine chromite ore with chromium oxide not exceeding 52% & Silica exceeding 4%.	3.00
Chromite lumps containing Chromium Oxide not exceeding 40%.	1.00
Beneficiated chromite concentrates (feed grade to be less than 33%).	No ceiling

Actual exports during last two years have been as follows:

Year	Quantity (in lakh tonnes)	Value (Rs. in crores)
1996-97	3.02	137.00
1997-98	2.70	106.00

Installed Capacity and Utilisation

There are 35 large and medium size units (including four 100% EOUs) with an installed capacity of 1.3 million tonnes (including 2 lakh tonnes of Charge Chrome capacity of four 100% EOUs). Besides this, there are small scale units having an installed capacity of about 1.80 lakh tonnes per annum.

Ferro alloy industry is a highly power intensive industry. High power tariffs, coupled with relatively poor quality of supply is one of the major reasons affecting the production and profitability of ferro alloy industry. Average consumption of power per tonne of different bulk ferro alloy ranges between 2700-4065 kwh in the case of ferro silicon. Due to this, the capacity utilisation in the industries has been in the vicinity of 50% to 55%. The production of ferro alloys indirectly related to the plan of production and growth of steel industry. The production of major bulk ferro alloys and Noble ferro alloys during last five years was as under:

Year	Quantity (In lakh tonnes)
1993-94	4.70
1994-95	4.78
1995-96	5.73
1996-97	6.94
1997-98	7.91*

Refractories

Refractories are the primary materials used in the internal lining of industrial furnaces and are classified from the chemical composition angle into-Acid Refractories, Basic Refractories and Neutral Refractories. In steel industry refractories are used for lining of coke oven batteries, blast furnaces, steel production furnaces, reheating furnaces, electrical arc furnaces etc. With the technological changes in the steel industry, the major thrust has been on economising on the use of the materials and improving technology in each area of operation/process where refractories are being used. The gradual phasing out of open hearth furnaces, adoption of continuous casting route and modernisation of secondary steel making processes, have lessened the demand for conventional refractories and increased demand for high performance refractories. In general, it can be said that all these improvements have resulted in lowering specific consumption of refractories per tonne of steel.

Export of ferro alloys

Export of ferro alloys from India have been showing an upward trend as may be seen from details given below:

Year	Quantity (In lakh tonnes)	Value (Rs.in Crore)
1993-94	1.68	251.56
1994-95	1.74	257.26
1995-96	1.90	451.55
1996-97	2.11	407.92
1997-98	2.59	504.55

Production of refractories during the year 1997-98 is given below:

Refractory Item	Production (M.T.)
Firebricks and Shapes	172193
High Alumina bricks and shapes	240138
Silica bricks and shapes	38471
Basic bricks and shapes	202106
Special Products	17427
Others	39075
Total	7090410

The import of refractory items in 1997-98 stood at 27804 tonnes while exports were of the order of 9770 tonnes. In value terms, export during 1997-98 was Rs.20 crores.

6

Survey and Exploration

Survey and exploration

The Geological Survey of India (GSI), a premier Earth science organisation in the country, has been rendering services to the nation and the scientific community at large in meeting the geoscience information requirements in diverse fields, natural resource build–up and the country's multifarious developmental missions. In the post–Independence era, there has been an added emphasis on locating and harnessing the natural resources for meeting the growing demands of various developmental sectors such as mineral/metal, power (thermal, hydro and nuclear), agricultural, irrigation, transport and communication, etc. Management of risks caused by natural hazards such as floods, landslides, earthquakes, defining and delineating areas prone to environmental degradation and providing geological inputs to optimise sustained development in the rural and urban sectors are gradually becoming important functions of the Survey.

The upgradation of geoscientific expertise through training and induction of modern technology and sophisticated tools coupled with R&D efforts also received attention. Creation of computerised database for management of geoscientific information and dissemination to the user agencies, both Government and private sectors, has become an important activity of the organisation. These activities of the Survey have benefited almost all the major segments of the Indian economy

The functions of the Geological Survey of India encompass a wide spectrum of earthscience activities such as geological, geophysical and geochemical mapping, specialised thematic studies, ground and airborne geophysical surveys, marine surveys, geoenvironmental studies, geotechnical and seismotectonic surveys and various laboratory studies.

The thrust areas of GSI's activities have evolved with the changing national priorities throughout the last eight Five Year Plans and are presently oriented in the light of the objectives and goals set for, the 9th plan. GSI has moulded its role suitably in tune with the economic reforms and liberalisation measures introduced during the period.

The Airborne Mineral Survey and Exploration (AMSE) Wing of GSI is engaged in airborne geophysical survey for the preparation of geophysical maps. The geophysical data sets are followed up by ground evaluation aimed at prospecting and exploration of minerals (including oil/hydrocarbon resources).

The Marine Wing of GSI continued off–Shore geoscientific surveys with the help of deep sea going research vessel, R.V. Samudra Manthan and two coastal research vessels, R.V. Samudra Kaustubh and R.V. Samudra Shaudhikarna, the latter two being deployed within the territorial waters along the East and West coasts respectively. The near shore areas within the bathymetric depth of 0–10m, where coastal research vessels cannot manouvre, were surveyed by hiring small mechanised boats and utilising portable equipment.

Mineral exploration

Mineral search and appraisal by the Geological Survey of India was tailored to meet the thrust areas envisaged for the 9th Plan with particular stress on prognostication for gold, diamond, basemetal and platinum groups of minerals.

Dimension Stone Granite (DGS) has of late assumed great importance due to its ever increasing demand in the export market. Accordingly, GSI has formulated the Phase – 11 programme (1997–98 to 2000–2001) with a more comprehensive objective to cater to the demands of this expanding industry,

During 1998–99, a total of 167 programmes on mineral investigation were taken up. Region–wise breakup of these programmes is given in the following table :

Minerals	*ER*	*NER*	*NR*	*SR*	*CR*	*WR*	*AM–SE*	*Total*
1	*2*	*3*	*4*	*5*	*6*	*7*	*8*	*9*
Coal/Lignite	14	–	–	5	13	4	–	36
Non–Ferrous minerals	2	1	2	–	3	11	2	21
Strategic & rare minerals	4	–	2	4	–	–	–	10
Gold	5	3	6	21	12	5	2	54
Diamond	2	–	–	5	3	–	–	10
Precious & Semiprecious minerals	–	–	–	–	–	1	–	1
Ferrous minerals	3	–	–	1	3	–	–	7
Limestone/ Dolomite	–	2	–	–	–	3	–	5

(Contd. . .)

Other Ind. minerals	2	–	1	3	1	1	–	8
Dimension stone	3	1	2	5	2	2	–	15

Geoscientific survey

Systematic geological mapping

The programmes on systematic mapping, however, did not get priority during the 7th and 8th Plans because of shifting priorities and shortage of required manpower to take up the additional work after fulfilling the prioritised programmes. Moreover, the areas left for systematic geological mapping are mostly unapproachable areas of the North–Eastern region, in the States of Arunachal Pradesh, Manipur, Nagaland, Mizoram and Meghalaya; of the northern Himalayas in the States of Jammu & Kashmir and Uttar Pradesh; Jarwa inhabited islands of Andaman & Nicobar; Abhujmar Plateau of Madhya Pradesh and parts of Andhra Pradesh. The output/coverage of this activity in many of these areas, has been aided by the support of airphotos, IRS imageries and digital image processing. The areas, so covered, however, will not be taken as mapping coverage on 1:50,000/63,360 scale but the information and findings of PRS inputs will be incorporated in compilation of quadrangle sheets.

The status of systematic geological mapping is given in the following table :

Specialised thematic studies

The multidisciplinary specialised thematic studies in selected areas were initiated a decade ago. The stress was laid on integrated inputs backed up by laboratory studies/analysis. This activity, in addition to resolving the problems on specific themes, is serving as the first logical step towards demarcation of potential mineralised zones outside the well defined areas.

(in thousand sq. km.)

Formation area mapped	*Total*	*Total Area area*	*Hard Rock Mapped*		*Quaternary area*	
			Total	*Total area*	*Total mapped*	*Total area*
Total area	3287.00	3083	2386.00	2206	901.00	877
Unappro–achable area	141.20	–	123.60	–	17.06	–
Mappable area	3145.80	3083 (98% approx.)	2262.40	2206 (97.94%)	883.40	877 (99.27%)

Airborne surveys

The programme of airborne surveys of GSI has three components:

i) Multisensor Surveys with the Twin Otter aircraft of GSI.

ii) Aerogeophysical data processing.

iii) Ground evaluation of Airborne Geophysical Survey data.

Under the 15 year National programme with NRSA, GSI has covered 73% of the total target of 18,43,380 sq. km. by aeromagnetic survey till 1996–97.

Upgradation of the data acquisition and processing systems is going on as per schedule with training of scientists at Scintrex, Canada.

Marine survey

The Marine wing of the Geological Survey of India carried out cruises within the Exclusive Economic Zone (EEZ) by R.V. Samudra Manthan (RVSM). Within the territorial waters of the Bay of Bengal and the Arabian sea R.V. Samudra Kausthubh and R.V. Samudra Shaudhikama (RVSS) undertook surveys.

During the said period, RVSM surveyed in the regions west and east of Andaman Islands falling in the Bay of Bengal and the Andaman Sea, respectively. A total of 3015 Ikm (line kilometre) and 2765 Ikm of bathymetric and magnetic surveys respectively were carried out against a target of 1880 Ikm each of bathymetric and magnetic, respectively. Samudra Kausthubh covered 800 sq.km. against a target of 1000 sq. km. covering 350 Ikm of bathymetric and 150 Ikm of sub–bottom profiler against a target of 250 Ikm each in single cruise in the month of April, 1998.

Samudra Shaudhikama covered 1600 sq. km. against a target of 1200 sq. km. and covered 175 Ikm of bathymetric against a 220 Ikm target during the month of April '98 off Kundopur in the Arabian Sea.

Performance during 1998-99

Targets for the year 1998–99 (April 98 – March 99) and the achievements for the period April 98 – Dec. 98 and performance during the two previous years are indicated in the following table :

Mineral aearch & evaluation

Item		*96–97*	*97–98*	*98–99(+) Achieved upto Dec.'98*
Large Scale	T	3118.00	3945.90	2785.15
Mapping (sq.km.)	A	4048.00	4374.70	2928.46
Detailed	T	50.15	50.78	49.83
Mapping (sq.km.)	A	37.48	34.684	50.02
Drilling (metres)	T	1,47,698.00	1,28,210.00	89,810.00
	A	74,594.00	86,885.80	60,533.16

Survey and mapping

Airborne surveys

Item		*96–97*	*97–98*	*98–99(+)*
Multisensor Surveys by GSI Twin Otter aircraft	T	25,000 (12,500)	20,000 (10,000)	11,000 (5,500)
(LKM/sq.km.)	A	18,746 (8,861)	3219	**Nil

Marine surveys (sq.km.)

Item		*96–97*	*97–98*	*98–99(+)*
Mapping in EEZ beyond territorial waters by R.V. Samundra Manthan	T	23,000	*78,000	As the Systematic Survey within EEZ has been completed only parametric studies are being taken

taken up

up

(Contd...)

	A	23,000	67,664	
Survey in territorial waters by two	T	2,000	*3,600	2200
coastal launches	A	2,190	2,256	1900

Ground

Surveys (sq.km.)

Systematic	T	8,760	6,300	2507.60
Geological Mapping	A	7,542	3530	430.00
Specialised	T	7,148	7,430	7001.60
Thematic Mapping	A	6,649	4989	2775.00

Survey programmes

In connection with the multisensor airborne survey, an area of 9844 sq.km. encompassing 20,343 line km. of flying, was done over parts of Chattisgarh basin and in Betul district in two sectors, to locate kimberlite pipes and basemetal.

Mapping of an area of 57,324 sq.km. was carried out by R.V. Samudra Manthan in five cruises within the EEZ of India.

Systematic geological mapping of 430 sq.km. was carried out. Besides, specialised thematic studies on a large number of programmes were continued during the period under review.

Mineral search and evaluation

In connection with mineral investigation and evaluation, 2928.46 sq.km. of large scale mapping, 50–02 sq.km., of detailed mapping, and 60533.16 metres of drilling was achieved against the targets of 2785.15 sq.km., 49.83 sq.km. and 89,810 metres, respectively.

Coal and lignite

The national resource inventory as on 1.1.98, based on the data accrued through drilling by GSI and other agencies, indicated a total of 206.23 billion tonnes of coal. The all–India reserve of lignite stands at 29.36 billion tonnes as on 1.6.98.

GSI, during 1997–98 made a preliminary assessment of coal bed methane in Birbhum and North Karanpur coal fields based on in–situ reserves of coal and observed possible gas content. The total gas–in–place reserves amount to 1.64 trillion cu.ft. (Birbhum 0.87 billion cu.ft. and eastern part of North Karanpura 0.77 trillion cu.ft).

Gold

In the southern part of Dhanjori basin, search for gold in the QPC (Quartz Pebble Conglomerate) was intensified with induction of drilling. Detailed mapping and channel sampling were carried out in Sanudor block of Haludbari–Brauniya–Sanudar sector. The QPC is persistent over 450m strike length. Channel samples collected so far from Haludbari sector indicated an average grade of 0.75 g/t Au(gold).

Some of the prominent occurrences investigated have yielded a tentative additional reserve of 0.70 m.t. of 7.20 g/t Au in Dona East block, Jonnagiri belt, Kurnool district, Andhra Pradesh. A probable reserve of about 0.63 m.t. ore with an average grade of 3.54 g/t Au has been tentatively estimated in Chikkanahalli south block, Chitradurga belt, Chitradurga district, Karnataka. In Dugocha block in Manpura–Sanjela area, Dungarpur Dist., Rajasthan, geochemical sampling indicated gold values ranging from 0.12 ppm to 1.10 ppm in carbonate rocks. Significantly higher values of 2.09 ppm to 4.41 ppm Au have been recorded in the metavolcanic enclaves within the carbonates sequence. In Gurhar Pahar East Block, drilling carried out so far has intersected a number of mineralised zones analysing 0.5 to 1.0 g/t Au over width ranging from 1m to 16m. In Jammu & Kashmir, a programme of preliminary stream sediment sampling for placer gold and PGE was taken up in Taklung–Halne area, Leh district, Ladakh around the Kyun–Tso ultramafic body. In Sonadehi prospect Madhya Pradesh, the borehole SD–1 has intersected a 4.6m wide zone analysing 11.76 g/t gold at 1 g/t cut off. In Maharashtra several gold investigations were carried out in different prospects of Pular–Parsori Gold belt. viz. MaruparPular–Kosari block, Parsori East block, Parsori West block, and Pular (west) – Kosari–Kolari–Bhaonri and Ranmangli areas, Nagpur district. The Sonadehi prospect of M.P. and

Dona East block Jonagiri belt, Kurnool dist, AP seem to be promising.

Diamond

Regional search for kimberlite in basal Chhattisgarh Formation and the surrounding Saraipalli area, Raipur district, was taken up. Ground evaluation of aerogeophysical anomalies in parts of Raipur district and adjoining districts of Orissa are being continued during 1998–99 period for locating mineral targets including kimberlite. In Maharashtra, a multidisciplinary programme of search for kimberlite and lamproites was taken up in parts of Chandrapur, Nanded and Godchiroli districts. In Andhra Pradesh, two investigations were undertaken for search of new kimberlite bodies in the granite greenstone belts in Central segment of Wajrakarur Kimberlite Field (WKF), Anantapur district and Closepet Granite in the Kalyandurg area, Anantapur district, A.P. Three new kimberlite pipes (KL–1,2,3) have been, identified within Closepet granite in Kalyandurg area. A micro–diamond has been recovered from KL 2 body. Bulk samples from Anumpalle (P–10), Dibbasanipalle (P–11) and Golapalle (CC–4) kimberlite bodies from the Central segment of WKF were processed. So far, 24 diamonds weighing 3.58 ct were recovered by processing 659 tonnes of material from the Anumpalle body. A total of 225 tonnes of kimberlite material from Dibbasanipalle body was processed and two diamonds weighing 2.15 ct. were recovered. The Golapalle body produced 15 diamonds weighing 2.28 ct. from the processing of 88 tonnes of material. In Orissa, search for kimberlite/ Lamproite pipes in Indravati basin, Koraput and Nawarangpur district led to the identification of a number of prominent linements and a zone of high magnetic permeability near the northern margin of the basin.

Other minerals/metals

Mineral Commodities	*Reserve Estimated/ Significant finding*	*Areas*
1	**2**	**3**
Lead–Zinc–Copper	0.35 million tonnes of ore with 2.25%	South Sindeser Ridge, Dariba Pb+Zn.
Bethumni belt Rajasthan.		in
	1.14 million tonnes of ore with 3.82%	Latio–Ka–Khera East block of Pb+Zn. Dariba belt in
Bethumni Rajasthan.		
Manganese	0. 13 m. of Mn ore over a strike length of 220m and upto a	Parsoda block, Nagpur district Maharashtra depth of 30m.
Iron	Grab sampling of Iron ore indicated 56% to 68% Fe.	IOG of Sumdargarh and Keonjhar
Platinum Group of Metals (PGM)	Chromite–ferrochromite breccia in gabboioc matrix, traced for 100m length with PGM content upto 7.88 ppm.	Bula Nuasalin arera, Keonjhar district, Orissa
Dimension Stone	1700 cubic meters of dimension stones (coloured grantie)	Cuttack, Dhenkanal Angul, Deogarh and Sambalpur district, Orissa.

Geoscientific survey

Marine Survey

	Target of 98–99	*Achivementss upto Dec. '98*
1	2	3
Coverage in EEZ (sq.km.)	As the systematic survey has been completed only studies will be taken up.	within EEZ parametric
Coverage in territorial waters (sq.km.)	2200	1900
Ground Survey		
Systematic Geological Mapping (sq.km.) on 1:50,000 scale	2507.60	430
Specialised Thematic Survey (sq.km.) on 1:25,000 scale	7001.60	2775.00

Specialised investigation

Geotechnical investigation

The association of the GSI in major civil engineering projects of the country continued during the year. Geotechnical services were rendered to 34 projects involving about 303 investigations mostly sponsored by different State Governments, majority of which are related to water resource development projects.

Geoenvironmental investigation

.2 The GSI carried out 54 items on environmental studies, majority of them pertaining to regional geoenvironmental appraisal. Some were oriented towards the environmental impact assessment of specific anthropogenic activities. Some others are related with coastal geodynamics and some were oriented towards seismotectonics.

The 9th Plan proposal of the GSI envisages programme of Development of Village Economy through Mineral Resources Appraisal (DOVEMAP). The study includes assessment of quaternary and recent deposits, comprising boulder, pebble, sand and clay which may be utilised for building and construction purposes. The programme has so far covered 199 villages in the States of Assam, Tripura and Meghalaya. Shallow level drilling also will be taken up, wherever needed, to assess the low value high yield mineral/material resource and ground water pollution.

Studies have also been undertaken for the arsenic pollution in groundwater of several districts of West Bengal. In this regard, collaborative project has been taken up with Indian Council of Agricultural Research and IIT, Kanpur. The geoenvironmental appraisal in parts of Calcutta Metropolitan District, a CMDA–GSI joint investigation, was continued.

Geothermal studies

Investigation to study the recovery/extraction possibility of Cs (cesium) in the field has commenced in July 1998.

In view of location of a large number of thermal springs in most seismically sensitive zones in the U.P. Himalayas, a programme for monitoring thermal manifestations in seismically sensitive zones like Gangnani in Bhagirathi Valley, Tapoban in Alakananda Valley, Deobata in Kali Valley has been proposed.

A MNES (Ministry of Non–conventional Energy Sources) sponsored project for assessment of power potential and direct heat utilisation possibilities from geothermal resources in Northern and Central India was taken up. Compilation of data is under progress.

Seismotectonic studies and natural hazards

GSI undertook investigations on seismotectonics with the aim to compile necessary database for assessment of seismic hazard potential of different parts of the country. With this view, the compilation of seismotectonic Atlas of India on 1: 1 m scale has been taken up and is in an advanced stage of finalisation.

The World Bank sponsored DST (Department of Science and Technology) project for setting up of the Khandwa telemetered network is progressing well. GSI has also been entrusted with the setting up of a broadband seismic observatory at Jaipur by DST.

At the request of Government of Maharashtra, GSI actively interacted with the Earthquake Rehabilitation Wing of Maharashtra for preparation of a seismic hazard map of Maharashtra in collaboration with Lamont Doherty Earth Observatory, U.S.A.

Laboratory and research

Laboratory studies including Research and Development activities in different disciplines of geoscience, constitute essential and integral components of most of the programmes/projects of GSI. To generate a database through laboratory studies and related research investigations, sophisticated analytical capabilities and infrastructural facilities in the disciplines of Petrology, Mineralogy, Geochemistry, Geochronology, Isotope Geology, Palaeontology, Photogeology, Remote Sensing and Geophysics have been developed. Linkage between the field investigations and optimum laboratory support needed for execution is built up in each of the schemes/ projects. In addition to the service programmes, the laboratory based divisions have taken up R&D programmes. Some of the findings in research investigations are as follows:

Petrological research has been oriented towards (1) granite–granulite relationship and crustal evolution of Chhotanagpur Gneissic Complex, (2) petrological studies of the Anorthosite massifs of Chilka, Orissa, for comparison of similar rocks in Antarctica and (3) evaluation of petro–tectonic implication of the granulitic suites, north of the Sausar Belt in the over all context of the tectono–thermal evolution of the Central Indian Mobile belt. A modest beginning in the field of experimental petrological studies has been made through a collaborative project with Allahabad University on lamproites of the Bokaro Coal Field.

In the field of Palaeontological studies the find of metazoans activity suggests thigmotactical locomotion, digging and tunnelling in the glauconite standstones of the Semri Group which indicates the appearance of metazoans to be at least 1100 m.y., contrary to the existing perception of 860 m.y.

Finding of post canines of tritheledontid cynodont in the Carnian Tiki Formation from where the earliest mammal was discovered is particularly significant because it underscores the validity of the tritheledontid – mammal transition rather than the trithylodontid – mammal hypothesis.

Study of cephalopods from the Jurassic of Kutch made it possible to demarcate the Bathonian–Callovian and Callovian–Oxfordian boundaries.

Geochronological and related isotope research was undertaken in southern Granulite terrain, peripheral areas of Bundelkhand Complex; Champanar Group of rocks of Eastern Gujarat and Mishmi Diorite Complex of Arunachal Pradesh.

Elagiri syenite and Alangeyarn syenite in Southern Granulite terrain yielded Ca 850 Ma age which coincides with the younger alkaline plutonism of the Eastern Ghat, Mobile Belt.

The age of the granite intruding the Parsoi Formation (Mahakoshal Group) in southern UP along the Narmada lineament suggests the upper limit of the age of Mahakoshal metasedimentary rocks to be older than 1.7 Ga.

In Gujarat, the granite intrusives into the Champanar Gneiss yielded an age of 950 Ma and the pre–Champanar Gneiss has shown the metamorphic age around 1200 Ma. This age indicates closer affinity to the rock suites of Central India, rather than those of the Aravallis. The Mishmi Dioritic Complex of Dibang Valley, Arunachal Pradesh, indicated the Mesozoic crystallisation age of 142+9 Ma with low initial Sr ratio. This Mesozoic age indicates a probable relation with the Karakoram Granite Complex.

Chernical laboratories of GSI have analysed 92,835 samples involving 8,81,357 determinations.

Information dissemination

Dissemination of geoscientific information through various publications, thematic maps etc. forms a very important domain of the GSI's activity.

During the period under review, thirty five publications were brought out and nine more are in different stages of printing.

Twenty five Quadrangle geological maps were printed bringing the total number of published Quadrangle sheets to 172 out of a total 284 sheets amenable to geological data collection and publication. Geological and Mineral Map of North East India on 1:2 million scale and one sea–bed map of Territorial Waters of India in parts of Bay of Bengal have also been released this year. The Geological Map of India on 1:2 million scale has been published.

Computerisation effort in GSI gained momentum since June, 1996 with the commencement of the major project of "setting up of the Geoscientific Data Centre in GSI" in collaboration with the BRGM, France. The project has provided necessary input in modernising the map production facility of GSI at Hyderabad and Digital Image Processing facility at Nagpur, besides setting up of state–of–the–art geoscientific data centres at Calcutta, Lucknow, Nagpur, Hyderabad and Jaipur. The Centre for study of Ore deposits and Metallogeny (CSOM) has also been set up under the project at Jaipur.

The National Data Centre will serve as the nodal information window for the geoscientific community and commercial entrepreneurs. Human resource development forms an integral part of this on–going project and 50 officers have been trained in specialised subjects for running different centres and broadening the expert base in the organisation.

As a part of the post–GSI–BRGM project and in conformity with the National IT policy, GSI has embarked upon an ambitious programme on Informatics aimed at launching multiple database programmes at different locations to achieve faster growth of digital database.

The collaborative programme between the GSI and several Indian institutes and organisations for creation of database of multi–themed georeferenced data for parts of Madhya Pradesh and Maharashtra is progressing well.

GSI has taken up a programme for creating a database on earthquakes recorded in India and adjoining countries covering 00–370 N latitudes and 680–980 E longitudes. Thematic earthquake hazard and probability maps on selected tectonically active areas have been generated.

Training

The Training . Institute of GSI with its centres located at different parts of the country imparts training to professionals from the GSI and State/Central Government Department, PSUs and some foreign countries. It conducts about 28 programmes per annum.

International participation

GSI continued co-operation with international organisations, as in previous years, through participation in bilateral and collaborative programmes, various geoscientific projects under CGMW (Commission of Geology and Map of World), UNDP (United Nations Development Programme), SAARC (South Asian Association for Regional Cooperation) etc. and acted as the nodal agency for IGCP (International Geological Correlation Programme) in India.

GSI – BRGM, France collaboration programme involved upgradation and development of professional skills in GSL Now it is taking a turn towards supply of equipment like drill rigs. The possibility of Indo-Vietnam, Indo-China and Indo-Canada collaboration in selected fields is being explored. A collaborative proposal with Mauritius for mapping of their EEZ is under consideration.

Several fields like assistance in improvement of analytical facilities in GSI, supply of ground geophysical instrument, etc. have been identified for collaborative venture between India and Australia. Collaboration with South Africa is on the anvil. The GSI participated in the Indo South African Working Group meeting held in South Africa during August, 1998.

Under the existing Indo–Bhutan cooperation programme, GSI continued to render services in the fields of geological survey, mineral exploration, geotechnical investigation for hydroelectric and communication projects.

In order to fulfil the aim of effective manpower development, GSI organised 19 (nineteen) training courses on core disciplines and management.

During 1998–99, twenty two scientists went abroad for specialised training/attending seminars and eight officers participated in international seminars/ symposia held in India.

Expedition to antarctica

The GSI participated in the XVII Antarctica Expedition with a two member team. An area of about 1000 sq. km. was geologically mapped on 1:50,000 scale in eastern part of Muhlig–Honffmanfjcela between long. 6^0 30'–7^0 E and Lat. 71^0 40' – 72^0 S. It is also participating in the ongoing XVIII Antarctica Expedition.

Mineral exploration corporation limited

The Mineral Exploration Corporation Limited (MECL) was set up on 21.10.1972 to undertake detailed systematic mineral exploration and allied works in order to establish reserves of various minerals/ores in the shortest possible time so that the large time gap entailed between the discovery of a prospect and its eventual exploitation could be curtailed. The Corporation has been carrying out these functions by steadily enlarging its volume and scope of activities during the last 26 years and has so far established about 86,671 million tonnes of reserves of various minerals, besides estimating 471 billion cubic meters of coalbed methane resources in 7 coalfields in India.

MECL is the premier exploration agency in the country now. It carries out exploration activities under two major heads (a) Promotional, on behalf of Government of India, in which the projects are funded by Central Government on the basis of detailed exploration schemes formulated by the Company, in the perspective of demand vs. availability as well as national priorities and (b) Contractual, on behalf of other agencies including Public Sector, Private Sector and State Government, as per contract executed by MECL with them. The company is also diversifying into commercial mining of selected minerals and coal sampling to increase its revenue.

With its Headquarters at Nagpur, MECL has been carrying on operations all over the country. The activities of the company are carried out through separate divisions formed for attending to specific functions. The operational divisions comprise, Geology, Drilling and Mining. Support services are provided by Finance Division, Materials Management Division, Personnel & Administration Division ' Commercial Division and Planning & Monitoring Division. It also has a full fledged Information Technology Centre at Nagpur.

Physical performance

The production of drilling & mining, and the submission of geological reports during the year 1998-99 vis-a-vis previous three years are given below:

Production	*1956-96 Actuals*	*1996-97 Actuate*	*1997-98 Actuals*	*Target for 1998-99 (Budget estimate)*	*1998-99 Actuals upto Dec. '98*	*1998-99 estim-ated (Revised estimate)*
1	2	3	4	5	6	7
Drilling (Mtrs)	1,60,626	1,80,261	1,75,551	2,00,000	1,55,502	2,00,000

(Contd...)

Mining (Mtrs)	2,079	3,758	5,215	5,500	3028	5,000
Final Geological Reports (Nos.)	50	65	71	40	45	–

Financial performance (operating results)

(Rs. in crores)

Details	*Actuate for the Previous 3 years.*			*Annual Budget Estimates*	*Actuals 1998-99 Upto*	*Annual esti-mates*
	95-96	*96-97*	*97-98*	*1998-99*	*Dec'98*	*1998-99 (Revised Estimate)*
Income	35.40	41.15	51.58	63.50	42.09	63.50
Operating Cost	41.41	38.34	49.39	58.34	38.37	56.45
Interest and transaction loss	3.38	4.03	0.94	6.96	0.64	1.00
Depreciation and amortisation	2.93	2.94	3.71	5.00	2.96	5.00
Net profit before income tax and dividend	-12.32	-4.16	-2.86	-6.80	0.12	1.05

Sales performance

Details	*Actuate for the Previous 3 years.*			*Annual Budget Estimates*	*Actuals Upto Upto*	*Annual esti-mates*
	95-96	*96-97*	*97-98*	*1998-99*	*Dec'98*	*1998-99 (Revised Estimate)*
Sales	35.40	41.15	51.18	63.50	42.09	63.50

Ongoing projects

The priority in exploration continues to be for energy minerals i.e. coal and lignite. In addition, exploration for lead, zinc, copper, molybdenum, uranium, gold, iron ore and diamond was also continued.

Under the promotional programme, exploration is in progress for the following :

Promotional exploration on behalf of the department of mines

a) Copper at Kalapahar and Singhana in Rajasthan
b) Bauxite at Amtipani-Dipakujam block in the state of Bihar.
c) Copper at Dhadkidih in the state of Bihar.
d) Molybdenum at Vellampatti in the state of Tamil Nadu.

Priority regional exploration for coal and lignite on behalf of the ministry of coal

a) Coal in the command areas of Singareni Collieries Company Ltd. and Coal India Ltd. in CCL, SECL & WCL areas)
b) Lignite in the states of Tamil Nadu. Rajasthan & Gujarat.

A brief review of major Exploration programmes undertaken during 1998-99 (Upto December '98) is given below :-

Coal : Major exploration activities of MECL continued to be for coal, in which exploration was continued on contractual basis on behalf of Coal India Ltd, and also on behalf of Ministry of Coal under priority regional exploration programme. Total 102,543 m. of drilling and 693 m of mining/mine construction work was completed in various blocks of Bihar, West Bengal, Madhya Pradesh, Maharashtra and Andhra Pradesh for Coal India Ltd. and

Singareni Collieries Company. Under Priority Regional Exploration programme on behalf of Ministry of Coal, against an allocation of 75,500 m for the year 1998-99, 48,761 m of drilling representing 65% has been completed.

Copper : Detailed exploration for copper Surahari block in Jhunjhunu dist., Rajasthan was concluded and geological report was submitted, establishing therein 4.960 million tonnes of copper ore reserves with average grade of 0.92% Cu. Drilling work is in progress at Kalapahar and Singhana blocks (Rajasthan) where 4843m of drilling has been carried out till Dec.'98.

Uranium : Mine construction work for Uranium was continued at Jaduguda (Bihar) as a contractual work for UCIL and 552 m. of mining was achieved during 98-99. Mine construction work at Narwapahar commenced, where 462 m of mining was carried out upto 'Dec.'98.

Lead-Zinc : Mine Construction work at Balaria, Mochia, on behalf of HZL (Rajasthan) was continued and 617m of mining has been completed upto Dec.'98.

Bauxite : Exploration for bauxite at Amtipani-Dipakujam, district Gumla. on behalf of Department of Mines, was continued . A total of 2,893 m of drilling and 115 m of pitting work has been achieved during the current year upto Dec.'98. The contractual work at Baphlimali on behalf of UAIL commenced during November '98 and 566 m of drilling has been achieved.

Iron Ore : Exploration work at Kudremukh Iron ore on behalf of KIOCL was concluded where 1,634 m. of drilling was carried out. Besides, developmental mining on behalf of OMC at Gandamardhan has also been completed during the year and 363 m of progress has been achieved.

Lignite : Exploration for lignite was continued on behalf

of Ministry of Coal under priority regional exploration programme and a total 55,000 m of drilling was allocated in the states of Tamil Nadu, Rajasthan, Gujarat and Maharashtra for priority regional exploration, against which 36,139 m of drilling has been completed in 1998-99 upto Dec.'98. Besides 250 m of drilling for lignite was completed on behalf of RSMDC. Thus, the total drilling achievement in lignite including contractual and priority regional exploration during 1998-99 is 36,389 m.

Gold : Exploration for gold was concluded in Chinmulgund Project with 1707 m. of drilling. Geological report was submitted establishing 1.36 million tonnes of gold ore reserves with 4.51 g/tonnes.

Significant findings based on MECL's endeavour

a) Total 2430 million tonnes of coal reserves were established (264 million tonnes of cooking coal and 2166 million tonnes of non-cooking coal).

b) 380 million tonnes of lignite reserves established in Sindhari and Gadiyala blocks in District Barmer and Bikaner, Rajasthan.

c) Total 5 million tonnes of Copper Ore reserves were established at Surhari copper deposit, Dist. Jhunjhunu, Rajasthan under promotional programme funded by Department of Mines.

d) 1.36 million tonnes of gold ore reserves with 4.51 g/tonnes of gold were established at Chinmulgund block district Haveri, Karnataka.

e) MECL has established fully equipped Remote Sensing centers at Ranchi and Patna on turnkey basis for Government of Bihar. The revenue generated on account of this activity stands at around Rs. 46 lakhs.

Expansion & diversification

In order to expand the activities of the company,

vigorous marketing efforts were made through competitive biddings and discussions/negotiations, besides entering into MOUs and collaborative programmes with different clients, within India and abroad. The results of these efforts, in brief, are as under:

- Three work orders, valued at Rs.479 lakhs were received from various clients during 1998-99, through competitive bidding. In addition, work orders for undertaking coal sampling for five washeries in CCL command areas have been received.
- Memorandum of Understanding signed with :
  - i) CSIR/CFRI for coal sampling and analysis work.
- CCL & SAIL, for coking coal sampling and analysis work for washeries at Kathara, Kargali and Rajrappa area.
- Discussions were held with
  - i) GIPCL-for taking up balance drilling work for lignite exploration and for developmental drilling in Vastan area.
  - ii) WCL-regarding coal sampling and analysis work at Nandan Washery.
  - iii) Central Material & Soil Research, Ministry of Water Resources for Geotechnical activities and related work. A brochure on Geotechnical endeavour was prepared and presented.
  - iv) HZL authorities regarding Geophysical work and also for detailed exploration of lead-zinc in Kayar block district Ajmer, Rajasthan. Exploration of Kayar block is

proposed to be taken up in collaboration with M/s.Boart Longyear, Canada.

v) RSMDC officials at Udaipur for Lignite exploration at Nagore, Rajasthan.

vi) ANETCO, Oman regarding consultancy work in Oman.

vii) BARC officials to undertake Remote Sensing studies in western Rajasthan and environmental studies in Bundelkhand region Stage-II, Phase-III. The revised cost estimate for environmental studies is being submitted and the work is likely to be awarded soon.

viii) BALCO representatives, for bauxite exploration at Bodai-Daldali, Dist. Rajnandgaon, M.P.

ix) Negotiations/discussions with SICON/VED for taping of CBM in Vidarbha, Maharashtra State is in progress.

x) Discussions were held with WCL authorities regarding coal sampling and analysis work.

➢ Agreement for Geological & Geophysical work at Deri block, Rajasthan, submitted to M/s.METMIN for ratification.

➢ Review of exploration for copper in Singhana block (Phase-II) was prepared and sent to Department of Mines, Government of India

➢ Nominated members participated in the different meetings held to organise the Mega Event of Department of Mines for celebration of the Golden Jubilee of Indian Independence.

➢ Agreement was signed with UCIL for excavation

or ore pass system for vertical shaft and other development work at Narwapahar Project.

- The draft MoU sent to IICT, Hyderabad for quality of Singareni Collieries despatched.

- **MECL participated :**

  i) MECL participated in the Seminar and Exhibition held at Nagpur from 06.08.98 to 08.08.98 on the occasion of the "Mega Event" organised by Department of Mines.

  ii) In Jharkhand Udyog Mela at Ranchi, from 9th to 13th, October, '98 organised by Chhotanagpur Small Scale Industry. Activities of MECL were exhibited through posters and multi media presentation.

  iii) In Metals & Metallurgy 1998 exhibition at New Delhi, from 7th to 10th October, '98, where activities and products of MECL were shown through posters, exhibits and multi media presentation.

  iv) In Exhibition "IMM-98 International" from 26th to 29th October, '98 at New Delhi. Highlights of MECL works and services offered were presented through trans slides to the multinational companies and investors.

  v) In an exhibition organised by Association of Exploration Geophysics (AEG) at Nagpur, from 28th to 30th October, '98. Highlights of MECL work specially of Geophysics were displayed through posters and multi media presentation.

  vi) In an international exhibition "Pride of India" at Hanoi, Vietnam, from 23rd to 26th October, '98. Highlights of MECL activities were presented to multinational companies and investors.

Programme for diversification

As a part of its diversification programme, MECL intends to enter into commercial mining of limestone, dolomite, silimanite and fluorite in the state of Maharashtra, in collaboration with Maharashtra State Mining Corporation (MSMC). So far the indications are positive and the proposal may be through in 1999-2000.

MECL has been identified as third party Agency for Coal Sampling and Analysis. MECL has already taken up Coal Sampling and Analysis work at Jarangdih for CCL-SAIL, at Korba and Baikunthpur for SECL-NTPC and at Dhanbad for BCCL-SAIL. From the identified quantum of work the expected revenue during 1998-99 would be around 50 lacs.

Energy conservation

Mineral Exploration Corporation Limited carries out exploratory drilling and mining for various minerals through different projects located at remote places of the country. The equipments used for exploration work are mainly driven by diesel engines. The electrical energy consumption for physical work at sites is practically at the minimum (e.g. lighting in mine face). The following steps are being continued in order to curtail the expenditure on POL and promote POL conservation.

a) Machineries/Vehicles consuming excessive POL are timely withdrawn from operations for overhauls/repairs.

b) MECL has set up Regional Maintenance Centre at Nagpur, Ranchi and Hyderabad for monitoring the conditions of machineries/vehicles deployed at projects. Regular/periodical maintenance of machineries/vehicles is being carried out to reduce consumption of fuel, breakdowns and improve performance.

Energy conservation is attempted in 2 ways:

Direct - by avoiding/minimising wastage :

All the drilling personnel have been advised to avoid/ minimise wastage of fuel, lubricants and other consumables.

Indirect - by carrying out periodical maintenance of all machinery and vehicles:

Regional Maintenance Centres have been set up at Nagpur, Ranchi and Hyderabad for monitoring the condition of the drills, machinery and vehicles deployed at various projects of the MECL for taking up their periodical and preventive maintenance for reducing breakdowns and improving their performance. This will help to reduce the consumption of fuel, lubricants, etc.

Computerisation

MECL has updated Computer Hardware and Software and a new Information Technology Centre to cater to the requirements of Fields and Corporate Office.

The technology upgradation in terms of procurement, installation and commissioning of latest Computer hardware and software was done. New Computers (Pentium) were installed at RMC's, Sr. Manager (Geology) Offices and user Divisions for computerised data entry and processing to improve upon efficiency and quality of work.

The computerised data processing related to geological modelling applications, geostatistical application, MIS, Salary, costing, Billing and other miscellaneous jobs continued during 1,998-1999.

Action taken on abatement of pollution and environment protection

The exploration activities of MECL do not cause any

pollution. However, MECL is carrying out Environmental studies for helping the exploitation agencies to plan measures for possible avoidance of pollution and environmental degradation at the time of mining. Baseline data is being collected for Environmental Impact Assessment (EIA) in various exploration projects and a report on the same is included in geological reports of the project. MECL has also taken up "Site Characterisation" studies for selection of suitable and safe places for disposal of hazardous wastes.

During the year 1998-99 MECL has submitted 3 reports on environmental studies.

1) Project Granite Bundelkhand Phase-II MP : Site characterisation studies for identification of suitable site for disposal of hazardous wastes.

2) Base line status of environment at Chinmulgund gold project, Dist. Haveri, Karnataka.

3) Project Granite Jaisalmer, Rajasthan. Site characterisation studies for identification of suitable site for disposal of hazardous wastes.

4) Base line environmental study is in progress in Mannargudi Lignite Project Tamil Nadu, Amtipani Dipakujam Bauxite Project, Bihar and Dhadkidih Copper Project, Bihar.

5) Remote sensing studies for Kutch and Saurashtra region is in progress.

6) Report on land use/land cover studies for Surahari-Kalapahar block was submitted.

7) Remote sensing report on Mohan block, Bander Coalfield, Dist. Chandrapur, Maharashtra was submitted.

Salient aspects of the work being done by advisory boards/ councils

During 1998-99, MECL participated in the 2nd "Standing Committee on Promotional Projects" (SCPP) formed by the DOM, held on 30.7.98 in which three proposals were approved for execution under promotional activity sponsored by the Government.

MECL participated in the 33rd Central Geological Programming Board meeting held during Sept. '98 at Calcutta. MECL programmes were reviewed in subcommittee meetings on coal/lignite, non-ferrous metals, noble metals, ferrous minerals, etc. held during the year.

MECL participated in the meetings of the State Geological Programming Board of Maharashtra, Kerala, West Bengal, Andhra Pradesh, Tamil Nadu and Gujarat and had close interaction.

Perspective oin non-ferrous metals

During 1998-99 (upto December '98) the company has carried exploration for copper ore and took part in target reach for lead-zinc ores. The details are given below:

Copper ore

i. The exploration for copper ore in Surhari block, Khetri copper belt, District, Jhunjhunu, Rajasthan was concluded in June '98 with completion of 4373 m. of exploratory drilling, 1.0 sq. km. of geological mapping and other associated jobs. The Geological report was submitted in October 1998. A total of 4.96 m.t. of copper ore reserves with 0.92% of Cu were established Kalaphar block, Khetri belt, Rajasthan is in progress. Against an annual work programme of 5600 m in these blocks, 1044 m has been achieved in

Singhana block and 2873 m in Kalaphar block. It is planned for intimation of work in Singhana block after completion of exploration in Kalapahar block.

Among the new projects

ii. The exploration for copper ore commenced in Dhadkidih Area, Singhbhum copper belt, Bihar in the month of July 1998 and work is in progress. The objective of the exploration is to confirm the strike and depth continuity of the lodes, static correlation and structure of lodes, estimates of reserves/grade and estimate beneficiation characteristics. So far, total of 5354 m of drilling has been completed upto December '98.

In the non ferrous sector, the annual work programme of MECL for the year 1998-99 includes 10,650 m of drilling for copper ore against which 10197m has been achieved upto December 1998.

Research & development activities

Following Science & Technology scheme is in progress :

1) Evaluation of metal content in basemetal and allied ores by geophysical logging.

– The administrative approval from the Department of Mines in respect of revised cost estimate for the project has been obtained vide letter no. 1(17)/86 - Met.-IV (Vol-II) dated 10.9.97. This is for supporting the expenditure to be incurred by MECL to undertake the commissioning of the imported equipment procured under this scheme.

– Full commissioning of the equipment by M/s Scintrex, Canada. The firm offer from the company has been obtained. The equipment shall be dispatched for upgradation at M/s Scintrex by the end of February '99

– Against the grant of Rs. 53.06 lakhs received during 1998-99, the sum of 23.06 lakhs would be utilised for this scheme.

New schemes

– Further, three new S&T proposals were put up in the SSAG meeting held on 19.12.97, New Delhi.

– The Committee has approved the scheme entitled "Development of electromagnetic tomography and buried electrode method for geotechnical studies and mineral exploration". Administrative approval for the scheme from DOM has been received vide letter No. 14(25)/96 Met-IV dated : 12.02.98. Out of the Rs. 53.06 lakhs received for S&T project during 1998-99 Rs. 30 lakhs shall be utilised for purchase of equipments for which specifications of equipment have already been collected. The global tender has been floated in January '99. The tender would be opened by March '99.

– In respect of other two schemes viz. (i) Development of geoenvironmental evaluation system (GENES) and development of model data bank/model for geo-friendly mines for selected minerals/ mining districts and (ii) Conceptual geological ore body modelling of Gadag Gold Field, Karnataka, the committee directed to re-submit the schemes after discussions with different organisations and necessary modifications.

– A meeting was held at Nagpur, as per the directives of SSAG, for review and modification of the scheme of "GENES" and development of model data bank/model for geo-friendly mines for selected minerals/mining districts. Experts on environment from GSI and IBM participated. The modified scheme is being put up to DOM.

Industrial relations

As per the approval of the Department for pay revision, the pay and allowance of Executives under IDA pattern effective from 1.1.92 have been implemented with effect from 1.7.98 which has boosted the morale of front line executive and reduced the gap between CDA and IDA executives.

Contingent workmen of Bhopalpalli KTK-5A Project were on illegal strike w.e.f. 16.7.98. However, due to intervention of RLC(C)/ALC(C), Hyderabad, the contingent workmen called off the strike and have resumed their duties with effect from 21.8.98 and normal work has started at Bhopalpalli KTK-5A Project. The period of strike from 16.7.98 to 20.8.98 has been treated as "No work No pay" basis.

Pay Revision of all IDA executives (including Board Level) is due from 1-1 -1997 and Wage Revision of Unionised Regular employees is due from 1-4-1997. The Board in its 138th meeting held on 9th September, 1998 has approved payment of adjustable Interim Relief @ 10% of the basic pay subject to a minimum of Rs. 280/- per month to all I.D.A. employees on the roll of the Company, which is being paid.

At Chinoor Project Office, about 30 to 35 Ex. Contingent Workmen retrenched from MECL earlier, held demonstrations from 06.10.98 to 11.10.98 and also gheraoed the Project Office. Their main demand was regularisation of their services as per the CGIT, Jabalpur Award. MECL officials at the project explained the current status of the award and informed that the matter was subjudice as such and requested that they refrain from agitations, but they could not be persuaded. They continued their agitation from 13th to 16th October '98. Meanwhile, our officers met Mandal Revenue Officer, Chinoor on 13.10.98 and apprised him of the position. Mandal Revenue Officer, held discussion with these Ex. Contingent Workmen and requested them to call off their agitation immediately and not to precipitate since the matter was already subjudice. However, his request was turned down by these persons. On 14.10.98, ALC (C) and Labour Enforcement Officer, Mancherial also visited our project and held discussions with MECL officers at Chinoor. The matter was explained to him and he was requested to intervene in the matter so that the agitation was withdrawn. Accordingly, both ALC(C) & Labour Enforcement Officer, Mancherial requested them to withdraw their agitation immediately. On the request of the team of officials from CHQ and RMC Hyderabad, ALC(C), Mancherial visited the Chinoor Project Office on 16.10.98 and held prolonged discussions with the representatives of the agitating persons and they were impressed to withdraw the agitation/gherao immediately. They were agreed that MECL, can commence its operation from 19.10.98. It is worthwhile to mention that the regular employees of the Chinoor Project did not support or participate in this agitation and also had shown exemplary courage in dealing with the situation.

Perspective plan for women's welfare

We stand for raising and improving the socioeconomic status of women. For this purpose, we provide them training to acquire new skills for their career development. We also propose to organise programmes to educate women against social evils like dowry, regionalism, communalism, etc. depending upon availability of funds.

Welfare of tribals and minorities

Welfare of SC/ST's : MECL has given due importance to meet the socio-economic needs of the tribals and minority communities living in and around each camp/project site. However, in view of continued financial constraints being faced by the Company, no welfare activities were undertaken during the period under review. However, if any proposal for minor welfare activities is received for the upliftment of the weaker sections of the society, the same will be considered on the merits of each case keeping in view the fund availability.

Special recruitment drive for SCs & STs Keeping in view the difficult financial position of the Company and the surplus manpower, it has been decided to keep all recruitments including under "Special Recruitment Drive" in abeyance.

Personnel position as on 31.12.98 including SC/STs

The overall representation of SC/ST in MECL is 21.98% as on 31.12.98 and representation of SC/ST is as under:

Group	*Approved Strength*	*Total no. of Employees*	*SC*	*ST*	*% of SC*	*% of ST*
1	2	3	4	5	6	7
A		433	63	21	14.55	4.85
B	600	72	10	3	13.89	4.17
C		1703	243	115	14.27	6.75
D		1090	156	114	14.31	10.46
Total	2500	3298	472	253	14.31	7.67

Overall Percentage of SC/ST -21.98%

Employment of SC/ST/EX-SM/PH/LDP/minorities as on 331.12.1998

Group ities	*Total*	*SC No. of*	*ST Emplo- yees*	*Ex-*	*Physi- Service*	*LDP cally men*	*Minori- Handi- capped*
Executives	505	73	24	03	01	–	43
Non-Executives	2793	399	229	25	11	–	257
Total	3298	472	253	28	12	–	300

Export/import performance

The Company is neither exporting nor importing any goods.

Mou rating of PSU's achieved

The MOU rating of the company for last four years is given in the table below :

Year	*Composite Score*	*Rating*
1994-95	4.55	Poor
1995-96	2.20	Very good
1996-97	2.15	Very good
1997-98	2.27	Very good

Progressive use of hindi in official work

In accordance with the policy of Government of India for extensive use of Hindi for official purpose, all out efforts were made for progressively increasing the use of Hindi in official work,

HINDI DIWAS/PAKHWADA was organised at CHQ and other establishments of MECL from 01-09-98 to 14-09-98. At CHQ, Nagpur various competitions were conducted to encourage the use of Hindi among employees. Many executives and non-executives participated in these programmes. Concluding function of Hindi Pakhwada and Hindi Diwas was held on 14-09-98 which was presided over by the CMD, MECL. He also distributed prizes to the winners of various programmes. CMD, MECL appealed to the employees to encourage the use of Hindi in official work and complimented the employees who had participated in various programmes during Hindi Pakhwada. The function was attended by a large number of employees.

Abbreviations

1.	AEG	–	Association of Exploration Geophysicists
2.	ALC (C)	–	Assistant Labour Commissioner (Central)
3.	BARC	–	Bhabha Atomic Research Centre
4.	BCCL	–	Bharat Coking Coal Ltd.
5.	CBM	–	Coal Bed Methane
6.	CCL	–	Central Coalfields Ltd.
7.	CFRI	–	Central Fuel Research Institute
8.	CSIR	–	Council of Scientific & Industrial Research
9.	DOM	–	Department of Mines
10.	GIPCL	–	Gujarat Industrial Power Corporation Ltd.
11.	HZL	–	Hindustan Zinc Ltd.
12.	IICT	–	Indian Institute of Chemical Technology
13.	KIOCL	–	Kudremukh Iron Ore Company Ltd,
14.	MOIL	–	Manganese Ore India Ltd.
15.	NTPC	–	National Thermal Power Corporation
16.	OMC	–	Orissa Mining Corporation

17. POL – Petrol & Other Lubricants
18. RLC (C) – Regional Labour Commissioner (Central)
19. RMC – Regional Maintenance Centre
20. RSMDC – Rajasthan State Mineral Development Corporation
21. SAIL – Steel Authority of India Ltd.
22. SECL – South Eastern Coalfields Ltd.
23. SICOM – State Industrial Corporation of Maharashtra
24. UAIL – Utkal Alumina Industries Ltd.
25. UCIL – Uranium Corporation of India Ltd.
26. VED – Vidarbha Economic Development
27. WCL – Western Coalfields Ltd.

7

Public Sector

Steel Authority of India Limited (SAIL) (Excluding Subsidiaries)

Steel Authority of India Ltd. (SAIL) is a Company registered under the Indian Companies Act, 1956 and is an enterprise of the Government of India. It operates and manages five integrated steel plants at Bhilai (Madhya Pradesh), Bokaro (Bihar), Durgapur (West Bengal), Rourkela (Orissa) and Burnpur (West Bengal), a plant of the Indian Iron and Steel Co. Ltd., which is wholly owned subsidiary of SAIL.

SAIL has also four Special and Alloy Steels and Ferro-alloys units at Durgapur (West Bengal), Salem (Tamil Nadu), Chandrapur (Maharashtra) and Bhadravati (Karnataka). The plants at Chandrapur and Bhadravati belong to the Maharashtra Elektrosmelt Limited and Visvesvaraya Iron and Steel Limited respectively which are also subsidiaries of SAIL. The IISCO-Ujjain Pipe and Foundry Company Ltd., a subsidiary of IISCO, was manufacturing Cast Iron Spun Pipes at its works at Ujjain (Madhya Pradesh), is under liquidation. Besides, SAIL has seven central units viz. the Research and Development Centre for Iron and Steel (RDCIS) ' the Centre for Engineering and Technology (CET), the Management Training Institute (MTI) all located at Ranchi, Central Coal Supply Organisation located at Dhanbad, Raw Materials Division, Growth Division and Environment Management Division all located at

Calcutta. SAIL Consultancy Division (SAILCON) functions from New Delhi. The marketing of products of SAIL plants is done through the Central Marketing Organisation (CMO), Calcutta which has a countrywide distribution network.

Finance

The authorised capital of SAIL is Rs.5,000 crores. The paid-up capital of the Company was Rs.4,130.40 crores as on 30th September, 1998 which was held to the extent of 85.82% by the Government of India and the balance 14.18% by the financial institutions/GDR-holders / banks/ employees/individual etc.

Turnover and profit

The Company recorded the sales turnover of Rs.14624.07 crores in 1997-98. The post-tax net profit for the year 1997-98 was Rs.132.99 crores. The Company had declared a dividend of one percent on the paid-up equity share capital for the year ended 31st March, 1998. Government of India has received Rs.35.45, crores as dividend on its equity contribution in SAIL for the year 1997-98.

The Gross margin (profit before depreciation and interest) and net loss for the half year ended 30th September, 1998 was Rs.797.77 crores and Rs.616.91 crores respectively. The company recorded a sales turnover of Rs.6794.01 crores during the period. The Company during 1997-98 has raised Rs.767 crores through issue of Bonds to various financial institutions, banks, trusts etc. through private placement for financing Company's modernisation and other capital schemes. The Company further issued Bonds valuing Rs.570 crores during the period April-September, 1998.

Under the Public Deposit Schemes of the Company, the net deposits (i.e. net of repayments and renewals) as on 31st Match, 1998 stood at Rs.2520.25 crores. The net deposits as on 30th September 1998 stood at Rs.2467.70 crores approximately.

Capital expenditure

The Company incurred capital expenditure of Rs. 1955 crores on Fixed Assets and Capital Work-in-progress in the year 1997-98 and approx. Rs.996 crores during the period April-September, 1998 which have been primarily financed through borrowings from external sources.

Production performance

The four integrated steel plants of SAIL at Bhilai, Bokaro, Durgapur and Rourkela ended the year 1997-98 with an output of 11.62 million tonnes of hot metal, 10.3 million tonnes of crude steel and 8.71 million tonnes of saleable steel. Alloy Steels Plant and Salem Steel Plant recorded best ever production of saleable steel at 331 thousand tonnes.

The details of production plan and achievement for 4 integrated steel plants and 2 Alloy steels plants during 1997-98 are as follows :

(In Million Tonnes)

Item	Target	Actual	Fulfilment
Hot Metal	12.20	11.62	95
Crude	11.45	10.30	90
Saleable Steel	9.60	9.04	94

Energy conservation

The continued emphasis on energy conservation measures helped further in reducing energy consumption per tonne of crude steel for the 11th successive year and reached a level of 8.28 G.Cal/tcs during 1997-98. During the period April-September, 1998 energy consumption was almost of the same level.

Production Performance: 1998-99 (April-Sept 98)

The details of production plan and achievement during 1998-99 (April-September 1998) was as follows :

Item	Target	Actual	Fulfilment (%)
Hot Metal	5.63	5.38	96
Crude Steel	4.99	4.70	94
Saleable Steel (including ASP&SSP)	4.35	3.95	91

There was continued thrust during 1997-98 on improvements in techno-economic parameters. Coke rate in Blast Furnaces was reduced to 594 kg. per tonne of hot metal in SAIL four plants. The productivity of Blast Furnaces in SAIL plants was 1.25 T/m^3/day during 1997-98.

Development of small scale /ancillary industries

The Company continued to give encouragement to the development of Small Scale and Ancillary Industries. During 1997-98, value of stores and spares items purchased from these units was of the order of Rs.145 crores. During the period April-September, 1998, Rs. 64 crores worth of stores and spares were purchased from Small scale and Ancillary Industries.

Captive power generation

Captive power generation in SAIL during 1997-98 was average of 451 MW, which met 56% of the Company's total power requirements. Captive power generation during the year April-September 1998 stood at an average of about 440 MW as compared to 438 MW during April-Sept.97.

Environment Management

During the year 1997-98, two more Pollution Control Action Plan schemes were completed, bringing the total number of schemes completed to 109. Consequent upon the various pollution control measures implemented, ambient air quality and effluent discharge quality at various SAIL plants and townships are steadily meeting the norms. The stack emission compliance level has improved to 96 percent during the year.

Several training programmes, aimed to sensitize SAIL collective towards environmental awareness, have been conducted throughout the year, at various locations.. Sustained efforts have been made to green the SAIL plants, mines and townships with plantation of over 5.5 lakh saplings during the year 1997-98.

Sales and marketing performance

Industrial production during 1997-98 was at a rate slower than the previous year. During the year, the product-mix was constantly reviewed and adjusted to make it market oriented. Various specific segments like construction, tube-makers, furniture, etc. were identified and supplies were made in the customised sizes to match their exact requirements. The long term relationship with the major customers in the form of Memorandum of Understanding (MoU) yielded benefits in terms of better customer satisfaction and also helped to retain the company's customer base.

Sales

During 1997-98, the total sales of saleable steel by SAIL was at 8.1 Million Tonnes. In addition about 0.69 Million Tonnes of Pig Iron was also marketed. Steel products namely, plates, HR sheets, coils, semi, Cold Rolled Products and Wire Rods and Pig Iron worth Rs. 1087 crores (about 1.0 million tonnes) were exported, amongst others to U.S.A, Nepal, Sri Lanka and European countries during 1997-98.

During the period April-September, 1998, the total sales of saleable steel was 3.96 Million Tonnes. In addition 0.25 Million Tonnes of pig iron was also marketed. The export during this period was 256.7 thousand tonnes.

Capital schemes

The Company incurred a capital expenditure of Rs. 1955 crores during 1997-98 on fixed assets and capital work-in-progress, which has been financed through market borrowings.

The modernisation of Durgapur Steel Plant (DSP) has been completed during 97-98. Major thrust was given on stabilisation of production and achievement of rated capacity. Benefits have started flowing in and are expected to increase further in future years. Production has picked up and has shown a growth of 5 per cent in Hot Metal, 9 per cent in Crude Steel and 15 per cent in Saleable Steel as compared to 96-97.

At Rourkela Steel Plant the various global and indigenous packages under Phase-II Modernisation were in the final stages of completion. The balance works in modification of Hot Strip Mill and Reheating Furnace of Hot Strip Mill was progressing. Trial production has started at SMS-2- Continuous Caster at RSP.

At Bokaro Steel Plant major production facilities of Modernisation Eke both Continuous Casting Machines, Steel Refining Unit and Coiler-4 were installed. Trials of Coiler-3 was under progress. Balance works for Mill proper was nearing completion, Modification of Reheating Furnace-3 to Walking Beam Furnace, and Coal Dust Injection system to BF-4 were under progress.

At Bhilai Steel Plant Modernisation of Rail & Structural Mill (Stage I - Phase I) was commissioned. Oxygen Plant-II expansion and Twin Hearth Furnace

No.4 was in the final stages of completion. Work in Sinter Plant-3 and Cold Dust Injection system for BF No.6 were in progress.

With the completion of modernisation schemes, substantial improvements are likely to take place in terms of techno-economic parameters, particularly, specific energy consumption, coke rate, etc. besides better quality and increase in production capacity of saleable steel.

As a part of Government's initiative for development of North-East, a Hot Dip Galvanising Line of annual capacity of 40,000 tonnes is being set-up at Dagaon, Assam for which site activities have started.

Research & development

Research & Development Centre (R&D) of the Company pursued 208 R&D projects during 97-98. The projects provided technological input to SAIL plants/units with a thrust on cost reduction, value addition, quality improvement and development of new products. 102 projects were completed successfully. Out of these projects some of the noteworthy ones were:

- Quality improvement of Bhilai Rails,
- Continuous casting of CRNO grade steel at RSP,
- Yield improvement of Alloy Steels Plant concast slabs rolled at Salem Steel Plant,
- Development of energy efficient furnace burners,
- Evaluation of Coals for arriving at optimum blend.

Utilisation of completed R&D projects provided incremental improvement in the performance indices of plants. R&D Centre filed 3 foreign patents and 39 Indian patents in 1997-98. During 97-98,4 patents which were filed earlier, have been sealed by the Patent Office. The Centre also filed 16 Copyright proposals.

Raw materials

The Company met entire requirement of its iron ore and half of fluxes requirements from captive sources. SAIL Captive Mines produced 20.75 Million Tonnes of Iron Ore Lumps and Fines during 1997-98 and 9.69 Tonnes during the period April -September 98. Fluxes production was 2.65 Million Tonnes in 1997-98 and 1.58 Million Tonnes during the period April-September 1998.

In-House engineering

Centre for Engineering & Technology is continuing to provide design & engineering services to SAIL Plants and its Subsidiaries, in the area of Modernisation, Technological Upgradation and Additions, Modification & Replacement Projects. It has also started providing these services to other Steel Industry, both within the Country and Abroad. Some of the major Projects implemented during 1997-98. includes Modernisation of Rail and Structural Mill (Stage-I, phase-I) at BSP, Revamping of BF No.3 including installation of BIT at RSP and Mechanised Quick Work Roll Changing for finishing group at HSM of BSL. Most of the Projects are aimed at cost reduction and quality improvements. A large number of pollution control and automation schemes have also been engineered by CET.

SAIL Consultancy Division (SAILCON) continued to give thrust to establish SAIL as a leading Engineering and Management Consultant globally. SAIL has made its presence felt for provision of quality services in the domestic as well as international markets. Despite a low key investment climate during 97-98, orders worth over Rs.221 lakhs could be secured, out of which Rs.160 lakhs worth of orders were from foreign clients and about Rs.61 lakhs from Indian clients. This includes two prestigious order namely: Design, Engineering, Consultancy and Project Management Services for Englargement, Modernisation & Reconstruction of Blast

Furnace-3 of Egyptian Iron & Steel Company (EISCO), Egypt and a World Bank Project for Standardisation of Environment Monitoring of Air, Water, Noise and Formulation of Mitigation Plan for Coal India Limited.

Human resources management review

SAIL continued its efforts to maximise the contribution of the human resources in attainment of organisational goals. The thrust was on effective utilisation through concerted team working.

Manpower Utilisation

The manpower strength as on 31.3.98 to 30.9.98 was 1,76,147 (comprising 18,586 executives and 1,57,561 non-executives) and 1,70,289 (comprising of 17,890 executives and 1,52,399 non-executives) respectively. The manpower productivity was 96 tonne crude steel per man year during 1997-98.

Training

Training for developing the competencies of employees based on organisational requirements continued. During 1997-98, 83,769 employees were trained under on-going company-wide schemes. During April-September, 1998 37,590 employees were trained.

Employees' welfare

Various welfare 'Measures for the benefits of the employees, like free medical services (including extending mediclaim schemes to retired employees), housing, education for children, facilities of cooperative societies as well as providing avenues for socio-cultural activities were undertaken. On this account, the Company spent an amount of Rs.459 crores during 1997-98 and Rs.231.07 crores during April-September, 1998.

Sports

The Company persisted with its commitments of investing in youth particularly at SAIL townships in line with its Sports Policy of "Catching them Young". Special thrust was given to carry Top Sports to SAIL Townships for inspiring budding sports youth to play National Level game. SAIL Trophy of Cricket where in eight top Institutional Teams participated consisting of First Class Indian Cricketers and Test Cricketers was won by SAIL. SAIL Handball Academy at Bhilai was the only Sports Team invited from India at 50 years of Commonwealth Celebration at Edinburgh. Sub-junior and junior Teams from SAIL Townships won Gold Medals in Boxing, Athletics, Basketball and Handball in respective Nationals. Bhilai Team of Disabled Cricketers won the National Trophy defeating Bombay Team at Bangalore. SAIL Sports Scholars of Swimming, Chess, Archery and Rifles Shooting created new National Records in respective disciplines.

Industrial relations

Harmonious and congenial industrial relations atmosphere was maintained, through healthy on-going dialogue with trade unions and Officer's Associations and utilisation of different joint fora.

Safety

For motivating the employees to work safely, schemes of SAIL Safety award and Ispat Suraksha Puraskar were modified and a new scheme of Ispat Suraksha Puraskar for Mines was introduced during the year. Recent steps initiated to enhance safety performance of steel plants include cultivating a culture of safety, formation and functioning of safety circles, systematising safety audit, systematic safety inspection of Shop Floor on the basis of safety check fists, practising the concept of "Safety First", and motivating employees to fulfil their obligations towards safety.

Official language policy

The Company continued its efforts in the implementation of Official Language Policy of the Govt. of India. Emphasis was given to create an environment in which employees voluntarily adopt Hindi in their office work. SAIL's quarterly journal on Official Language 'Ispat Bhasha Bharti received wide acclaim from all quarters. Raw Materials Division, Calcutta & Bokaro Steel Plant were awarded prizes by the Deptt. of Official language, Ministry of Home Affairs for noteworthy implementation of Hindi.

Scheduled castes and scheduled tribes

The Presidential Directives on Scheduled Castes/ Scheduled Tribes continued to be implemented during the year. As on 31.12.97 Scheduled Caste and Scheduled Tribe employees were 15.11 percent and 11.20 percent respectively of the total manpower.

Peripheral development

SAIL has been playing an active role in undertaking various measures like providing drinking water facilities, health care programmes, educational facilities, recreational activities, etc. for the people living in areas near the steel plants/mines. A sum of Rs. 360 lakhs was spent on peripheral development during 1997-98 and Rs.60 lakhs (Prov) during April-September, 1998.

Awards

A team of three employees from BSP was selected for the Prime Minister's Shram Ratna Award. It is a matter of pride that this highest award, which is being conferred for the first time since inception, has been bagged by a SAIL team. In addition one employee from RSP was selected for Shram Vir Award during 97-98.

Total quality process

Steps have been taken to intensify the quality improvement drive in SAIL. During the year, the Merchant Mill and Wire Rod Mill of BSP, Cold Rolling Mill of BSL, Steel Melting Shop-I, Oxygen Plant-I & Oxygen Plant-II of RSP, Branch Transport and Shipping Office (BTSO), Vizag of CMO and Light Castings and Steel Foundry, Growth Division, Kulti Works also achieved ISO-9002 Certification. SAIL has also taken all appropriate steps for maintaining the ISO-9000 certified Quality Assurance systems in all its plants /units. As on 31st March, 1998, 31 facilities of the Company enjoy ISO-9001/ ISO-9002 certification.

Centre for Power Training Institute (CPTI), Rourkela, one of die unit of the company, has won the Golden Peacock National Quality Award in the Small Service Sector Category conducted by Institute of Directors, New Delhi for the year 1997.

Subsidiaries

The Indian Iron and Steel Company Limited (IISCO) owns and operates an integrated steel plant at Burnpur, captive iron ore mines at Gua and Manoharpur, captive collieries at Chasnalla, Jitpur and Ramnagore, a coal washery at Chasnalla and a large foundry complex at Kulti. The management of IISCO was taken over by the Government of India on the 14th July, 1972. Shares held by the private parties were acquired by the Central Government on 17th July, 1976. The shares held by the public financial institutions etc. were also purchased by the Central Government and subsequently all these shares were transferred to SAIL. IISCO became a wholly owned subsidiary of SAIL on 30th March, 1979. As a part of the physical restructuring of IISCO, the management of Kulti works and also the collieries and ore mines of the Company were taken over by SAIL in January, 1990 in terms of the Power of Attorney executed by IISCO.

Production performance

During 1997-98 the Steel Plant produced 782.4 thousand tonnes of Hot Metal, 405.8 thousand tormes of Pig Iron, 291.4 thousand tonnes of Crude Steel and 315.2 thousand tonnes of Saleable Steel.

(In '000 Tonnes)

	Plan	Actual	Fulfilment (%)
Hot Metal	840	782	93
Crude Steel	360	291	81
Pig Iron	422	406	96
Saleable Steel	377	315	84

Production Performance (Burnpur)-April-September, 1998

(In '000 Tonnes)

	Plan	*Actual*	*Fulfilment*
Hot Metal	362	382	105
Crude Steel	157	160	102
Pig Iron	175	186	106
Saleable Steel	159	145	91

Kulti works

Total Castings output during 1997-98 and April -September, 1998 was 47.9 thousand tonnes and 13.47 thousand tonnes respectively. Spun Pipes production was 21.3 thousand tonnes and 12.68 thousand tonnes during 1997-98 and April-September, 1998 respectively. Special emphasis was given for production of items required by Burnpur Works and other units of SAIL.

Collieries

Total coal raisings from three Captive Collieries was 721.9 thousand tonnes during 1997-98.

Ores mines

Iron Ore Lump production was 1046.7 thousand tonnes during 1997-98 from two Captive Ore Mines.

Capital schemes

During the year 1997-98 the Company incurred capital expenditure of Rs.25.75 crores on fixed assets and capital work in progress. Financial constrainst had affected the progress of on-going schemes and major new schemes were not taken up during the period.

At Burnpur Works Scheme for Augmentation and Betterment of Water supply system at Riverside Water Works had been completed. The pumping system along with all auxillaries were commissioned during the year.

A few small scheme like revamping of 16T E.O.T. Crane at Pig Gantry and modifications to Surge Bunker at C.H.P were completed.

At Kulti works, orders for Gas cleaning plants for Cupolas at LCD & SPP-3 were finalised and facilities are expected to be commissioned during the 1998-99.

Financial performance

During 1997-98 the Company achieved a turnover at Rs.909.08 crores. The net loss for the year after charging depreciation (Rs.25.98 crores) and interest (Rs.142.89 crores) was Rs.395.15 crores. Abnormal escalation in input prices, interest charges and lower sales price were major factors for the higher loss.

Company achieved sales turnover of Rs. 413.53 crores during April-September, 1998. During this period Company incurred net loss of Rs. 160.04 crores.

Steel Authority of India Ltd. provided Rs.1.63 crores for Capital Schemes and Rs.225.04 crores for Working Capital. SAIL provided additional loan of Rs. 9.62 crores during April- September, 1998.

As on 31st March, 1998, the Authorised Share Capital and Paid-up Equity Capital of the Company remained at Rs.550 Crores and Rs.387.67 Crores respectively.

Sales & marketing performance

Despite adverse market situation, during 1997-98 sales of 293.1 thousand tonnes of Steel (previous year 314.7 thousand tonnes) was achieved. Sales of Pig Iron were 298.0 thousand tonnes (previous year 256.7 thousand tonnes).

The Pig Iron market also showed declining trend because of which despensation was offered to match competitors landed price.

During April-September, 1998, 125.40 thousand tonnes of saleable steel and 131.45 thousand tonnes of pig iron were sold.

Exports

Export of steel materials during 1997-98 was 4320 MT to Nepal and export of Pig Iron of 3220 MT tonnes was to Bangladesh.

Environment management

Environment Management and Pollution Control have become priority areas in the activities of the Company. Environment Awareness Campaign through observance of World Environment Day and Environment Month was organised.

About 9,000 saplings of different plants were planted in Burnpur Townships and Works area. Workshops/Training on environment Management were organised for different sections of employees. Shop level core committee was formed at Coke Oven Department for Environment Management as per NJCS guideline.

Water consumption per tonne of Crude Steel was reduced from 13.78 m^3/t in 1996-97 to 13.06m^3/t in 1997-98. Stabilisation of Gas Cleaning Plant at Steel Melting Shop has been achieved. Vermiculture has been introduced for conversion of kitchen waste to compost manure.

Dust extraction system at Lime Calcining Department and Spun Pipe Plant No.3 at Kulti Works are under implementation.

Consent for air emission, effluent discharge and handling/disposal of hazardous waste has been received.

Human resources development

The Company continued to give great importance to the development of its human resources to improve efficiency and productivity

The manpower strength as on 31st March, 1998 and 30th September 1998, was 27,181 (comprising l, 334 executives and 25,847 non-executives) and 26,785 (comprising 1,310 executives and 25,475 non-executives) respectively.

During 1997-98 a sum of Rs.7.75 crores was received from National Renewal Fund for implementation of Voluntary Retirement Scheme and 483 employees were allowed voluntary retirement. Voluntary Retirement Scheme has been further extended for the year 1998-99.

Industrial relations remained normal and peaceful during the year.

The thrust towards Safety and Occupational Health continued. About 4,406 employees were trained on various safety and pollution control aspects during 1997-98.

The endeavour to make training more result and skill oriented continued during 1997-98 with 3,388 employees trained in various fields.

Scheduled Caste and Scheduled Tribe employees were 10.40 per cent and 1.18 per cent respectively of the total manpower as on 31.3.1998.

Welfare measures

Company undertook various welfare measure like maintenance of houses, education for children, medical facilities, socio-cultural activities and other facilities and spent Rs.40.59 crores during the year.

Official language policy

The Company continues to pursue vigorously the implementation of the Official Language Policy of the Government. Employees are encouraged to carry out their official work in Hindi and liberal incentives for such work are given. Official Language Fortnight Celebrations and workshops & Seminars on technical writing in Hindi were organised during the year. Rajbhasha Shields were awarded in the various competitions to encourage the employees. IISCO was awarded the Regional Shield and second best Town Official Language Implementation Committee (TOLIC) of Eastern Region 'C' shield for the year 1996-97.

Development of small scale/Anciliary industries

Procurement of Store and Spares from SSI Units is being made to the extent possible and orders were placed for about Rs.3.54 crores during 1997-98.

IISCO ujjain pipe & foundary Co. Ltd.

The Calcutta High Court by their order dated 10-7-1997 directed that IISCO Ujjain Pipe & Foundry Co. Ltd IISCO Ujjain) be wound up, and Official Liquidator was directed to take possession of its assets. Official Liquidator has already taken possessions of the assets and records of IISCO Ujjain.

Maharashtra elektrosmelt Ltd.

Maharashtra Elektrosmelt Limited is a subsidiary of SAIL situated in Chandrapur, Maharashtra and is a major producer of Ferro Manganese and Silico Manganese. It is also diversifying into other ferro alloys.

Financial performance

During 1997-98, the Company achieved the highest ever turnover of Rs. 18,997.45 lakhs and net profit before tax was Rs. 163.70 lakhs. The turnover and Net loss of the Company during April-September, 1998 was Rs. 80.33 crores and Rs. 12.75 crores respectively.

The Authorised Share Capital of the Company is Rs. 20 crores and Subscribed and Paid-up Capital is Rs. 10 crores. SAIL holding is approx. 98 percent of the paid-up capital.

Production performance

The production of all grades of Ferro Alloys during 1997-98 was as under:

(In Tonnes)

	1997-98
High Carbon Ferro Manganese	60391
Silico Manganese	33078

Production performance: 1998-99 (April-September)

(In Tonnes)

	Plan	1998-99	Fullfilments (%)
High Carbon Ferro Manganese	27074	25813	95
Silico Manganese	17648	17727	100

Research & development

Studies were carried out for control of dust emissions in SP-I and optimisation of MnOre/Flux sizes for improved performance of Sub-merged Arc Furnace (SAF) for Slag in Silico Manganese (SiMn) production.

For conservation of expensive Lumpy MnOre, 70% of Ore requirement has been replaced by sinters in SiMn production.

Environment

Environment Management and pollution control continued to get top priority in company's activities during the year. To keep environment clean for ecological protection, thrust was given in the areas of green belt development in and around the plant premises, solid waste management, monitoring of liquid and air effluent for various environmental parameters. In and around the Plant 3,000 teak and other saplings were planted in addition to the regular maintenance of existing 10,000 teak plants.

To comply with the environmental standards set up by Maharashtra Pollution Control Board, Gas cleaning plant for Sub-merged Arc Furnace-II (SAF-II) costing around Rs.1.6 crores has been commissioned. This would also enhance the availability of clean gas for gainful utilisation as a fuel to Sintering Plant and Lime Kiln. Gas based Captive Power Plant of 4.2 MW capacity for complete utlisation of clean gas has been approved and initial project activities has been started.

Continous steps were taken towards gainful utilisation of High Manganese Oxcide (MnO) Slag in Slag in Silico Manganese (SiMn) Production, Lumpy Slag in Silico Manganese (SiMn) Slag as rail ballast, Granulated Slag as stowing material in WCL mines and Sale of Slag in Silico Manganese (SiMn) Slag for road construction and repairs.

Sales & marketing performance

In order to meet the challanges arising out of the new economic policies and further liberalisation in import, measures were taken by the Company to find markets outside SAIL under the policy framed "Strategy for Managing Change".

The sale of different grades of Ferro Alloys during 1997-98 was 91,423 tonnes. There was sharp reduction in the price of Ferro Alloy products in international market. Therefore, no export has been made.

Human resources management review

The manpower strength as on 31.3.98 to 30.9.98 were 1050 (157 executives and 893 non-executives) and 1,040 (154 executives and 886 non-executives), respectively. As on 31st December, 1997, Scheduled Caste and Scheduled Tribes employees were 13.28% and 4.74% respectively of the total manpower. The industrial relations throughout the year remained normal. A total of 515 employees were trained during 1997-98.

Quality

After obtaining 9002 Certificate from Llyods Register of Quality Assurance (LRQA), Six Internal Quality Audits were conducted by the MEL Auditors, Two Inter Plant Audits were conducted by the SAIL Auditors and Two Surveillance Audits were conducted by LRQA. For Best System Control, 85 documents are in operation covering 18 departments. The entire Quality System was cleared for satisfactory maintenance without Non-confirmity Report (NCR).

Safety

During 1997-98 in Industrial Safety the Company was bestowed with "International Award" from the British Safety Council, National Award for the year 1993 and 1994 from the Ministry of Labour, Govt. of India, State

Safety Award from the council of Industrial Safety, Mumbai, for 1996 for longest accident free period, SAIL Chairman's Silver Plaque for no fatal Accident, Indira Gandhi Memorial National Award as Excellent Organisation by A.P. Central Sector Employees Federation, Hyderabad, and Regional Safety Award from Vidarbha Industrial Safety Committee for overall Safety Performance, use of Personal Protective Equipments and Safety Educational Training. MEL has been honoured by the Central Excise Department for distinguished record of payment of Central Excise Duties.

Visvesvaraya iron and steel limited

Visvesvaraya Iron and Steel Limited became a subsidiary of SAIL from 1st August, 1989 and it is situated at Bhadravati ' Karnataka. The Company is a major producer of special and alloy steels, On 23-3-1997, the company became a 100% subsidiary of Steel Authority of India Limited.

Financial performance

During 1997-98 and 1998-99 (upto September'98) the Company has recorded a turnover of Rs.210.28 crores and Rs. 121.38 crores respectively. The net loss during 1997-98 and 1998-99 (upto September'98) was at Rs. 83.87 crores and Rs.39.84 crores respectively. Slackening demand for alloy steels and pig iron in the market, higher imports of alloy and special steels, continuing liquidity crunch, substantial input cost escalation including power & fuel and upward revision of freight coupled with frequent power cuts and peak hour restrictions are some of the major factors responsible for the loss.

Production performance

The company produced during 1997-98 and 1998-99 (April -September), 129.57 thousand tonnes and 77.56

thousand Tonnes of hot metal and 30.9 thousand Tonnes and 23.8 thousand tonnes of Pig Iron, 50.4 thousand Tonnes and 25.38 thousand Tonnes of alloy and special steels and 6.7 thousand Tonnes and 4.0 thousand Tonnes of Ferro Silicon respectively.

Sales & marketing performance

Demand for Alloy & Special steels remain sluggish. Major sectors viz. Auto Forging Units and Engineering Industries continue to show no sign of improvement. Due to this market condition, some of the small producers of alloy and special steels have closed down their units and some are running with lower rate of production. During 1997-98 and 1998-99 (April-September, 98) alloy & Special steel sales were 49 thousand Tonnes and 26.7 thousand Tonnes respectively.

The drop in price of Pig Iron on account of drastic reduction in demand forced VISL to restrict production, as market prices were not remunerative. The Sales of Pig Iron in 1997-98 and 1998-99 (April-September) was 25 thousand tonnes and 27.6 thousand tonnes respectively.

Capital schemes review

The Company has completed the conversion of all the 10 Nos. furnaces (7 in HTS & 3 in Forge Plant) to Dual Fuel Firing System. One Tempering Furnace (TI) has also been converted to BF gas firing and one more annealing furnace is also being converted.

In order to comply with the stipulation of Karnataka Pollution Control Board, raising the height of 20 Chimneys have been completed and the balance work of one chimney is under progress.

Schemes for Technological Upgradation of main production facilities in VISL at an estimated cost of Rs.19.92 crores and installation of 7.5 MW gas based Power Plant at an estimated cost of Rs.21.69 crores are under implementation.

Human resources management review

Total manpower strength as on 31.3.1998 was 5,249 comprising of 559 executives and 4,690 non-executives and as on 30.9.98 was 5,125 comprising of 535 executives and 4,590 non-executives.

Percentage of SC/ST to total employment was 12.38 percent approximately as on 31.3,98.

For enhancing efficiency and skill of work force, the Company continued to give stress on imparting training to both executives and non-executives. With a view to reduce the surplus manpower, the Company has been taking several measures and accordingly under VR schemes, 334 employees took voluntary retirement during the year. National Renewal Fund has provided an amount of Rs.12.35 Crores for the Voluntary Retirement Scheme. Industrial relations continued to be cordial.

Official language policy

The Company has taken vigorous steps to implement the Official Language Policy of the Government. Many of the employees have joined the Correspondence Course in Hindi started by the Holding Company, SAIL. Suitable awards are given to all employees who pass the various examinations in Hindi conducted by SAIL.

Welfare measures

During the year 1997-98, the company spent an amount of Rs.5.27 crores on educational, housing, medical, social and other welfare needs of the employees.

Rashtriya Ispat Nigam Ltd. (Visakhapatnam Steel Plant)

Visakhapatnam Steel Plant the country's first shore-based plant and the sixth Public Sector Integrated Steel Plant had attained high levels of growth rate in production and superior technological norms within a short time. VSP with its superior quality of products established its presence both in the domestic and international markets. The plant was awarded the ISO 9002 for SMS and Downstream units covering all the products making it the first integrated Steel Plant to achieve this honour. VSP with its multifaceted superiority in quality, energy conservation and pollution control is harnessing its inherent potential to achieve the set goals by improving productivity, by upgrading the technologies, optimal investment and by judicious use of manpower.

Production performance

During 1997-98, VSP recorded production as follows: 3.16 million tonnes (mt) Hot Metal, 2.25 mt of saleable steel and 2.54 mt of liquid steel. VSP during Apr-Sep'98 achieved a production of 1.52 mt of Hot Metal, 1.26 mt of Liquid Steel and 1.10 mt of Saleable Steel which represents target fulfillment of 91% and 87% respectively. There has been 4% growth in the Liquid steel and Saleable Steel over the Apr-Sep'97. Production of Billets, Bars and MMSM products has also registered a growth of 2%,13% and 28% respectively over the corresponding period of last year. There has been increase in the production of value added steel from 1,14,605 tonnes during Apr-Sep'97 to 1,18,534 tonnes during Apr-Sep'98. The production performance of the first half of the year is given below:

April-September, 1998

(Unit 000' tonnes)

Product	Target	Actual	%Growth over prev. year
Hot Metal	1667	1524	-
Liquid Steel	1393	1262	4
Saleable Steel	1261	110	4

Techno-economic performance

VSP continued to improve its techno-economic parameters. During Apr-Sep'98 VSP achieved BF Coke rate of 499 kgs/thm against the target of 500 kg/thm. Average converter fife has also increased to 508 heats against budgeted figure of 500 and the average heat weight to 150.4 tormes against the budgeted figure of 150 tonnes. There has been continuous improvement in the yield of Bar and MMSM products surpassing budgeted levels. A record charging of nut coke to the extent of 53kg/thm during August, 98 was achieved to replace BF coke in Blast Furnace.

Marketing performance

Domestic sales of Steel Products during the first six months of 1998-99 were Rs.1, 151 crores compared to 966 crores during the corresponding year of 1997-98. Domestic Sales of Pig Iron has also increased to Rs. 14 crores compared to Rs.10 crores earlier. In the domestic market about 0.91 mt of steel was sold in 1998-99 as compared to 0.72 mt of steel sold in the first half of 1997-98.

The growth in the sale of Bar products was 29% and that of Medium Merchant & Structural Mills was 48%.

The economic crisis in the South-East Asian Markets and the large scale dumping of Steel of CIS countries affected adversely the export performance. As regards total sales there was a total growth of 6% in volume.

Inspite of sluggishness in the domestic market and the general recession, severe competition from other main and secondary producers and imports, VSP managed to retain its share in the market and sold about 1.03 mt of Steel in 1998-99 compared to 0.97 mt in 1997-98.

Financial performance

During 1997-98 VSP has registered a cash profit of Rs.280.22 crores after considering writeback of Rs.235.85 crores interest provided on Govt. of India loans during the earlier years. VSP registered a cash loss of Rs.69.13 crores against MoU target cash profit of Rs.61.31 crores for the period Apr-Sep'98. The net loss registered during the period is Rs.286.28 crores. The company has been making losses mainly due to the heavy capital related charges, the glut in the steel market and increase in the -cost of vital inputs such as coal and iron ore etc.

Power and mines

The power requirement of VSP is completely met from its own captive power generation sources. VSP is the first integrated Steel Plant in India to have entered into a MOU with the State Electricity Board for exporting power for a period of 3 years commencing from January 1997. During 1997-98 the net export of power to APSEB was 32 MW. This has increased to 40 MW during Apr-Sep'98.

Captive of mines of RINL at Madharam and Jaggayyapeta in Andhra Pradesh have registered a growth of 42.4% and 8.11 % respectively in production during Apr-Sep'98. Likewise Manganese mine at Garbham in A.P. registered a growth of 39.78% from Apr-Sep'98 compared to the corresponding period of 1997-98.

Pollution control and environment management

VSP has been according highest priority for preservation of the environment. Accordingly, sustained efforts arc continuing for controlling all emissions and effluents to keep up with the prescribed norms. Ambient air, stacks and effluents are being monitored daily as per the statutory norms and prompt actions taken to rectify any deviations observed.

A comprehensive study was made of all sources of phenolic spillages. Effective measures like recycling tar sludge in batteries, recycling spillages in by-products and providing oil collection pits etc. have been undertaken to maintain effluent quality within the norms. Recycling of solid wastes was taken up which led to the saving of raw material consumption.

Investment on Environment and Pollution Control:

	(Rs.in crores)
	1997-98
Total revenue expenditure in VSP	3463
Revenue expenditure on pollution control	85.6
During Apr-Sep'98, the revenue	41.72
expenditure on Pollution control.	(Prov.)

Safety

Safety has been accorded highest priority in VSP. Training in safety and remedial actions taken have led to reduction in the number of accidents over the years. Elimination of unsafe conditions, adoption of safe working practices and high standards of house keeping have been ensured. Safety committees have been formed for spreading safety consciousness among the employees. Contract workers are allowed to be engaged only after their training in safety. Regular and periodical safety inspections and supply of high quality personnel protective equipments have also been taken up.

Industrial relations

During 1998-99 a number of initiatives were taken up to promote and maintain cordial IR climate for smooth operation of the Plant. The collective bargaining system through joint Consultative Machinery was strengthened. Sporadic instances like sudden work stoppages, go-slow and pressure tactics have diminished due to the availability of JCM as an institutional channel for ventilating grievances and meeting the genuine demands of the employees. The elections for determining the majority union were held by Labour Department, Govt. of AT through secret ballot in June,98.

The elections were conducted peacefully and without hampering normal production activities. The issue of payment of bonus was settled by signing a Memorandum of Settlement with the recognised Union. The overall IR Climate during the period remained congenial as may be seen from low rate of absenteeism, minimum loss of mandays, peaceful elections and settlement of issues through negotiations and discussions.

Implementation of official language

During the year, 71 employees were trained in Hindi Prabodh and 29 employees trained in Hindi Praveen. 8 employees are undergoing training in Hindi Stenography. 2 Hindi Workshops were organised wherein 6 Executives and 25 Non-executives were trained. A Hindi Implementation Day was organised on 13.5.98. The employees of Town Administration, Medical, Training and HRD Departments have participated in this programme. Various Hindi competitions were organised for the employees and prizes were distributed.

Hindi Pakhwada (Fortnight) was also organised in VSP during the month of September, 1998. During this period various Hindi Competitions like Hindi Noting and Drafting, Essay Writing, Good Handwriting, Hindi Typewriting were conducted and prizes were given to the winners of the competitions in the Hindi Day Celebrations organised on 14.9.98.

National Mineral Development Corporation Limited (NMDC)

Incorporated on November 15, 1958, the National Mineral Development Corporation Limited (NMDC) is an undertaking of the Government of India engaged in the business of developing and exploiting mineral resources of the country (other than coal, oil, natural gas and atomic minerals). Presently its activities are concentrated on mining of iron ore limestone and diamonds. NMDC operates the largest mechanised iron ore mines in the country at Bailadila (Madhya Pradesh) and Donimalai (Karnataka). The limestone project is at Chawandia, Rajasthan and the Diamond Mine is situated at Panna (Madhya Pradesh).

Iron Ore

During 1997-98, NMDC produced an all time high of 14.59 million tonnes of iron ore. During the year 1998-99 (upto Sept.98), 6.10 million tonnes of iron ore has been produced.

Exports

Exports of iron ore produced by NMDC is canalised through the Minerals and Metals Trading Corporation (MMTC). Iron ore export is mainly to Japan, South Korea and China. In 1997-98 Export of iron ore stood at 7.2 million tonnesvalued at 516 crores. In 1998-99 (upto Sept.98), NMDC exported 3.03 million tonnes of iron ore valued at Rs.251 Crores approximately.

Domestic sales

During 1997-98 domestic sales of iron ore was 8.5 million tonnes. In the year 1998-99 (upto Sept.98) sale of iron ore to domestic consumers was 3.71 million tonnes.

Diamonds

During 1997-98, 30591 carats of diamonds were produced. In the year 1998-99 (upto, Sept.98) the production was 17,541 Carats.

Finance

The authorised share capital of the company is Rs. 150 crores. The paid up equity share capital was Rs.132.16 crores. Government of India loans outstanding are Nil.

Financial performances

The financial performance of the company for the year 1997-98 and 1998-99 (upto Sept.98) are given below:

(Rs. in crores)

Item	1997-98	1998-99 (upto Sept.98)
Sales/Turnover	757.69	383.85
Gross Margin	252.55	140.31
Profit/loss before tax	216.67	121.95

Disinvestment of shares of NMDC

The Government of India has disinvested shares of NMDC for the first time in the year 92-93. A total of 21.30 lakh shares representing 1.61% of the paid-up capital has been disinvested.

The disinvestment fetched the Government an average price of Rs.83.52 per share and maximum price of Rs.100/- per share against the face value of Rs.10/- per share. During the year 1997-98, 5,154 shares of Rs.10/- each have been disinvested in favour of the employees of the Corporation at the price of Rs.71/- per share. In the year 1998-99 (upto Sept.98) no disinvestment of shares were done.

Operating results

During 1997-98, the Company earned a profit of Rs.195.15 crores before tax. In the year 1998-99 (upto Sept.98) the Company earned a profit (before tax) of Rs.121.95 crores.

Recognition/Awards in 1998-99

Received Abheraj Baldota Environment Award for Environmental Protection and Sita Ram Rungta Memorial Award for Social Awareness for Bailadila Deposit-5 from Federation of Indian Mineral Industry (FIMI) at New Delhi on 29th July, 98.

Workers participation in management

The Scheme of workers' participation in management is working satisfactorily at all the three levels viz. Shop, Plant (Project) and Apex (Corporate) level. The meetings of the joint Councils takes place regularly and follow up action taken.

Capital schemes

Govt. of India approved the scheme of developing deposit-10/11A with a estimated capital cost of Rs.430.50 crores including foreign exchange component of Rs.18.61 crores. Project Implementation has been taken up and Equipment required for construction and mine development which were ordered have arrived.

These are deployed at Deposit-11A suitably for mine development work. Work in Deposit-10 could not be started since M.P.Government has given conditional clearance. Temporary working permission has been granted by MOEF and by State Government upto 17.06.99. In respect of Deposit-10 and Deposit-10 (Float Ore), MOEF has communicated the final approval to M.P. Government and the papers are under processing by M.P.Government Mineral Resources Department for renewal of lease.

Due to delay in getting the mining lease, the project is likely to be delayed as per present projection by approximately 22 months and the same is likely to be completed by June, 2001.

NMDC's Board of Directors in Feb. 95 approved setting up an Ultra Pure Ferric Oxide Plant at Visakhapatnam, A.P. at a cost of Rs.45.98 crores. The construction of this plant is in final stage. The Plant will be commissioned shortly.

New business development

As approved by the NMDC Board of Directors, a team visited Lalapur Silica Sand Project site and held negotiations with M/s.UPSMDC for evaluating the compensation. NMDC has submitted its offer with certain terms and conditions which has been accepted in principle by M/s.UPSMDC.

Exploration of gold in madagascar

A team has gone to Madagascar for study and discussion with the Government and other Mining Organisations. The team has recommended taking up exploration for Gold on priority. OMNIS a State Mining Corporation in Madagascar had accepted NMDCs proposal and given their consent for forming a joint venture with NMDC for exploration of Gold and other minerals. An MOU has been signed between NMDC and OMNIS, Madagascar for taking up the exploration -work. Arrangements are being made for setting up of office and commencement of work.

Research & development

The R&D projects are taken up in line with the Company's policies and programmes with a view to achieve optimum utilisation of mine wastes and production of value added products.

Highlights of R&D activities

New Technology/Process

- Creation of Pilot Plant Facilities and Process Development for Pigment Grade Ferric Oxide

- Commercial Plant for Production of Ultra Pure Ferric Oxide from Blue Dust.
- Development of process for production of synthetic Rutile & High Grade Ferric Oxide from Ilmenite concentrate obtained from Bhimunipatnam beach sands.
- Laboratory Study for Preparation of Caustic MgO from Panna Tailings and Panthal Magnesite.
- Development of Ferrite Powder mix from High Grade Ferric Oxide/UPFO
- Process Development for treatment of UPFO effluents
- Development of mineral Beneficiation process for production of High Grade. Ferric Oxide from powdery type of Iron Ore known as Blue Dust.

A Demonstration plant is in three shift operation, producing on an average 1,000 tonnes of High Grade Ferric Oxide of different grades. These products are being supplied to various manufactures of Ferrite components both in India and abroad, for market development.

Utilisation of mine waste

Setting up of Pilot Plant for Brick/Hollow Bricks from Kimberlite waste and its evaluation

Productivity improvement

With the implementation of Slime Beneficiation Plant, based on R&D studies, in the Iron Ore production mines, there is an increase in saleable Iron Ore production to the tune of 5 to 6% leading to increased productivity.

With the implementation of Perm-Roll magnetic separation technique, based on R&D studies, in the Diamond Processing Plant at Diamond Mining Project,

Parma, there is a substantial increase in production and productivity.

Development of new products

- High Grade Ferric Oxide for use in the manufacture of hard and medium soft Ferrite components.
- Ultra Pure Ferric oxide for use in the manufacture of soft Ferrite components
- Ferrite Powder Mix - A value added ready to use material for manufacture of Ferrite Components.
- Pigment Grade Ferric Oxide for use in Paint Industry
- Synthetic Rutile and High Grade Ferric Oxide from Bhimunipatnam beach sand.

Quality improvement programme

- Being a member of the Bureau of Indian Standards, participating regularly in updating the testing procedures to Ores and Mineraks.
- ISO Quality System is implemented and Certification Audit will be held in October, 98 for obtaining ISO 9001 accreditation certificate for R&D Centre. This is for the Quality Management System and for the Quality of Service/Product being offered by the Centre.

R&D expenditure

(Rs. in crores)

Year	Turnover	Expenditure on R&D	R&D Expenditure as % of Turnover
1996-97	649.39	5.94	0.92
1997-98	757.67	4.86	0.65
1998-99 (Upto Sept. 98)	383.94	2.25	0.59

Project status

No. of Projects in hand as on 1.4.98, viz.

- Process development for treatment of UPFO effluents
- Development of Ferrite powder mix for High Grade Ferric Oxide/UPFO.
- Creation of Pilot Plant facilities & process development for PGFO.
- Process development for production of Caustic Magnesia from Kimberlite waste.
- Setting up of Pilot Plant for brick/hollow blocks from Kimberlite waste and its evaluation.

No. of projects planned for 1998-99, viz.

- Utilisation of Accumulated iron ore slime.
- Setting up a commercial plant for production of Pig Iron from Bailadila Iron Ore Slimes adopting Romelt process of Russia.
- Setting up a Pilot Plant at Diamond Mining Project, Parma for manufacture of masonary bricks/hollow bricks.
- Setting up a Mini Pilot Plant for the manufacture of PGFO.

No. of Projects due for completion in 1998-99, 2, viz.

- Pilot Plant at Diamond Mining Project, Parma for the manufacture of Masonary bricks/hollow bricks from Kimberlite Tailings.
- Mini Pilot Plant for manufacture of PGFO.

No. of Projects completed in 1998-99.

Commercial Plant for production of Ultra Pure Ferric Oxide from Blue Dust.

Pollution control & environmental management

Actual Work Carried Out During the Year 1998-99 (upto Sept.'98) includes pollution control measures at:

- Bailadila iron ore project, Dep-5, Bacheli
- Bailadila iron ore project, Deposit-14/11C, Kirandul
- Donimalai iron ore project
- Parma Diamond Mining Project

Total Expenditure incurred for environment protection, upgradation and pollution control measures for all projects of NMDC are as follows:

(Rs.in crores)

Year	Amount Spent
1996-97	8.32
1997-98	11.43
1998-99 (upto Sept.98)	2.69

Mandovi pellets limited

Mandovi Pellets Limited (MPL), Goa is a joint venture company floated by Government of India through National Mineral Development Corporation Ltd. and M/s. Chowgule & Co. Pvt. Ltd. (CCPL), a Private Sector Company. The company has its pellet plant at Goa with an annual capacity of 1.8 million tonnes.

During the year 1998-99 (upto Sept.98) the company produced 2.96 Lakh tonnes of pellets and despatched 2.98 lakh tonnes of pellets. The company's income for the year 1998-99 (upto Sept.98) is Rs.3,206 lakhs which includes miscellaneous receipts of Rs.50 lakhs. After adjusting the operating expenditure of Rs.3,393 lakhs, depreciation of Rs.109 lakhs and interest of Rs.48 lakhs, the loss for the year 1998-99 (upto Sept.98) is Rs.344 lakhs.

Energy conservation

Consumption of Energy per tonne of Iron Ore Excavated

Electrical Energy -KW / Tonne of excavation

Year	Target	Actual
1996-97	2.85	2.21
1997-98	2.85	2.27
1998-99 (upto Sept.98)	2.22	2.47

Diesel Consumption - Ltrs./Tonne of Excavation

Year	Target	Actual
1996-97	0.32	0.30
1997-98	0.32	0.29
1998-99 (upto Sept.98)	0.28	0.31

The Consumption is likely to come down by the year end.

Projects implemented during 1998-99

- Extensive use of Fluorescent Lamps for all industrial uses.
- Installation of PF improving Capacitors and maintenance of PF at + 0.90.
- Installation of Non-Conventional Energy Sources like Solar Panels for water heating and cooking purposes in Guest House.
- Reduction in domestic energy consumption.
- Reduction of idling time of dumpers
- Recycling of Lubricants.
- Formulation of Energy Audit Teams and carrying out energy audits.
- Award schemes for best Suggestions.

J&K mineral development corporation limited

Jammu & Kashmir Mineral Development Corporation Limited (J&KMDC) as a subsidiary company of NMDC was incorporated on 19.5.1989 for development of various mineral projects in the state of Jammu & Kashmir. NMDC holds 74% of equity in J&KMDC, the remaining 26% is owned by J&K Minerals Limited, a State Government Public Sector Undertaking. The Dead Burnt Magnesite (DBM) Plant of 30,000 tonnes per annum was sanctioned by Govt. of India in Nov. 1992. But the project construction could not start since the viability of the project was badly affected due to reduction in customs duty on DBM in 1993-94 and further fall in the International price. NMDC intimated this to the Ministry of Steel on whose direction, further activities of the project were kept in abeyance pending establishment of the economic viability of the project. This matter was discussed in detail and it was felt that the project will not become economically viable and therefore it was decided to close the project in its original form for which Government approval was sought.

Subsequently, on the advice of the Government, it was decided in JK MDC Board in the meeting held on 23.12.97 to restart the project in a modified form in three phases as given below:

Phase-I Develop the deposit for a production of 25,000 MT of saleable magnesite in the first year at a capital cost of Rs.451.82 lakhs.

Phase-II Expand the production to 50,000 MT of saleable magnesite per annum subject to availability of market from the second year onwards.

Phase-III Expand the mine capacity to approx. 1 lakh tonnes and set up a 30,000 TPA DBM plant subject to economic viability based on the then prevailing market price for DBM.

The Board of Directors of J&KML and NMDC have also agreed to the above proposal and Ministry of Steel has been informed accordingly. Works are being taken up in the project in accordance with the above modified plan to start Phase-I. Tenders for development of approach road to the mine and construction of bridges and culverts are under evaluation. Action has also been taken for procurement of additional mining machinery and weigh bridge.

Kudremukh Iron Ore Company Limited (KIOCL)

The Kudremukh Iron Ore Company Limited (KIOCL), one of the country's largest 100% EOU, was established in April, 1976 to meet the long term requirements of Iran, An Iron Ore Concentrate Plant of 7.5 million tonnes capacity was set up at Kudremukh.

This project was to be financed in full by Iran. However, as Iran stopped further loan disbursements after paying US $ 255 million, the project was completed as per schedule with the funds provided by Government of India.

While the project was commissioned on schedule, consequent upon the political developments in Iran, they did not lift any quantity of Concentrate. As a diversification measure, the Government approved the construction of a 3 million tonnes per year capacity Pellet Plant in Mangalore in May, 1981. The plant went into commercial production in 1987 and is now exporting both Blast Furnace and DR grade Pellets to many countries including Turkey, Australia, Indonesia, China, Taiwan, Japan etc., and also to domestic Sponge Iron units such as Ispat Industries, Vikram Ispat..

Production

A target of 6.2 million tonnes and 2.9 million tonnes is set for production of Iron Ore Concentrate and Iron Ore

Pellets respectively during the year 1998-99. As against a target of 2.925 million tonnes of Iron Ore Concentrate fixed for the period April to September, 1998, the actual production was 2.560 million tonnes which represents 88% target fulfilment.

Production of Pellets during the period April to September, 1998 was targetted at 1.340 million tonnes and the actual production during this period was 1.045 million tonnes representing 78% target fulfilment. In addition to this, 26,850 tonnes of Pellet Fines were generated during the said period.

The reasons for shortfall in production of Concentrate and Pellets upto September, 1998 during the current year are as under:

- The Asian economic crisis has had a very serious impact on the Company. Reduction in Oil prices in the Middle East leading to lower consumption of steel and consequent reduction in the production of steel has adversely affected the shipment schedule of KIOCL's buyers viz., Iran and China. They have not been able to keep up their shipping schedules for lifting the contracted quantities. As a result, they have not been able to open LCs. This has led to a situation where KIOCL's stockyards are full forcing the company to stop production activities;
- Due to storage yard being full, KIOCL's Concentrate Plant and Pellet Plant had to be stopped during the current year 1998-99 as under:

Months	Concentrate Plant	Pellet Plant
April, 1998	—	8 Days
May, 1998	—	3 Days
June, 1998	10 Days	—

August, 1998	9 Days	8 Days
September, 1998	12 Days	8 Days

Continued power cuts and load restrictions imposed b, the State Electricity Board.

Highlights

The Captive Power Plant at Mangalore recorded the highest ever power generation of 16.743 million units during the month of August, 1998 surpassing the earlier record of 13.855 million units generated in February, 1998

Exports

During the year 1997-98, total shipments were 6.145 million tonnes comprising 3.315 million tonnes of Concentrate and 2.830 million tonnes of Pellets. For the year 1998-99, a target of 3.3 million tonnes of Concentrate and 2.800 million tonnes of Pellets has been fixed.

As against a target of 1,640 million tonnes of Concentrate and 1.380 million tonnes of Pellets fixed for the period April, 1998 to September, 1998, actual shipments were 1,333 million tonnes of Concentrate and 1.023 million tonnes of Pellets representing 81% and 74% of the relevant targets respectively. In addition to this, 32,134 DMT of Pellet Fines were shipped during the first half of 1998-99.

Total sales for the year 1997-98 were Rs.593.91 crores. Estimated sales for the year 1998-99 is Rs.625,26 crores. As against a target of Rs. 303.55 crores fixed for the period April, 1998 to September, 1998, actual sales were Rs.247.41 crores representing 82% of the target.

The Export earnings during the last five years from 1993-94 and upto September, 1998. during 1998-99 are detailed below:

(Rs. in lakhs)

Year	Concentrate	Pellets	Total
1993-94	21022	20647	41669
1994-95	16729	20205	36934
1995-96	20676	27172	47848
1996-97	21900	27359	49259
1997-98	23310	36081	59391
1998-99	10135	14606	24741

Financial performance

An overview of the performance of KIOCL during the year 1998-99 upto September, 1998 together with actual for the previous three years, is indicated below:

Particulars	1998-99 (upto Sept. 98)	1997-98	1996-97	1995-96
Total value of sales	24741	59391	49259	47848
Gross Margin	4269	14250	13040	13759
Total profit on account of operations of the year	1969	9151	8562	10585
Inventories (excluding finished stock)	12039	11763	11712	11776

Worker's participation in management

The Works Committee in the Plants of the company are functioning effectively and joint Plant and Shop have contributed to the improved industrial relation as well as workers' participation.

Safety measures

A Safety Department is functioning effectively. Pit Safety Committees with Workers' representative meet regularly to discuss various Safety Measures. Safe rules have been compiled for each work area, covering a safety aspects. All employees have been provided wit these is booklets. As is the practice, 'Safety Week' was observed during the year.

Manpower position

As on 30th September, 1998, the total number of employees in KIOCL were as follows:

Group	Total No.of employees including SC, ST as on 30th Sept., 98	SC in position	ST in position
A	477	56	12
B	302	12	01
C	1448	196	45
D	187	57	28
(Sweeper)	43	35	04
Total	2457	356	90

Progressive use of official language

The Company follows the directives issued by the Government of India regarding progressive use of Hindi for official purposes. Hindi teaching programmes for the employees are a part of training programme of the Company.

Cash awards and increments are given to those who perform well in these programme Company's House magazine is published in E Hindi and Kannada languages. Hindi Week was celebrated between September 14-20 1998 at all locations at Kudremukh, Mangalore and Bangalore.

Manganese Ore (India) Limited (MOIL)

Established in 1962, Manganese Ore (India) Limited (MOIL) is the largest producer of Manganese Ore in India. At the time of inception, 49% shares were held by the Central Province Manganese Ore Co. Limited (CPMO). The remaining 51 % were held in equal proportion by Govt. of India and the State Governments of Madhya Pradesh and Maharashtra. Subsequently, in 1977 the shares held by CPMO in MOIL were acquired by Govt. of India and MOIL became a wholly owned Government company with effect from October 1977. As on 31.3.1998, the Government of India held 81.57% shares in MOIL with State Governments of Maharashtra and Madhya Pradesh, holding 9.62% and 8.81% shares respectively.

MOIL produces and sells different grades of Manganese Ore. These are:

- High Grade Ores for production of Ferro Manganese,
- Blast Furnace grade ore required for production of Hot metal and,
- Dioxide Ore which goes into production of Dry Battery Cells.

MOIL has set up a plant based on indigenous technology to manufacture Electroytic Manganese Dioxide. This product is also used for the manufacture of dry battery cells.

Finance

Authorized capital of the company is Rs. 30.00 Crores. Paid-up capital was Rs. 15.33 Crores as on 31.10.1998.

Performance

The productivity (output per manshift in tonnes) during 1997-98 was 0.371 and 0.357 in 1996-97)

Conservation of energy

Consistent with the National Policy of conserving energy and also to contain the cost of production, the company has embarked upon an economy drive in this sphere, Various steps, including energy audit have been taken to conserve energy and minimise power consumption.

Repayment of Government loans

The Company repaid in full balance plan loans amounting to Rs.216.07 lakhs together with interest of Rs.28.37 lakhs to the Government of India thereby discharging its complete loan liability.

Progress of capital schemes/ implementations of projects

The work of renovation and enlargement of Hardy's Shaft upto 33 mtrs and further deepening and lining by 147 mtrs is in progress at Balaghat Mine.

Research & development and technology upgradation

MOIL has undertaken several Research and Development Schemes for technology upgradation and conservation and optimum utilisation of valuable mineral resources. These schemes detailed below were undertaken to cut down cost of production, improve productivity and safety.

- Use of Cable Bolting and Steel Roof Support in underground mines.
- Use of Sand Stowing in underground Mines in place of manual filling.
- Improvement in underground mining support methods including Geotechnical investigation and cavability studies.
- Diamond drilling to locate new Manganese beating areas and prove further reserves in the existing leasehold areas.

- Beneficiation of medium and low grade ores as well as medium grade dioxide ore to battery grade.
- Optimisation of process parameters for E.M.D.Plant.

Diversification plans

The Company has ambitious diversification plans to manufacture new products/value added products so that the Company can become a multiproduct organisation in the course of time. As a part of its diversification efforts the company has set-up/is implementing the following projects.

Electrolytic Manganese Dioxide Plant (EMD)

The 700 TPA capacity Electrolytic Manganese Dioxide(EMD) Plant set up as a part of diversification plan is working satisfactorily. The quality of the product is of international standard. The capacity of this plant has been expanded by 200 TPA considering good demand in the domestic market.

New EMD Plant

The work of preparing project report was awarded to MECON who have submitted their report. The same is being studied by the Company.

Ferro manganese plant- balaghat mine

The work of construction of 10,000 TPA Ferro Manganese Plant at Balaghat Mine at an estimated cost of Rs.570 lakhs has already started. The commissioning of the Plant is deliberately being delayed on account of unfavourable market conditions at present. However, trial production was started from October, 1998.

Captive power plant

Considering the increasing requirement of power at Balaghat Mine due to setting up of Ferro Manganese Plant and the restraints in power availability in M.P: the

Company is setting up 8 MW Captive Power Plant at Balaghat Mine at an estimated cost of Rs.21.80 crores. The Govt. approval is awaited. The preliminary work is in process.

The Company is also examining the possibilities of setting up a High Intensity Magnetic Separation Plant and a jigging Plant.

Cost reduction plans

The company has introduced several cost reduction measures some of which are as follows :

- Improvement in productivity.
- Proper manpower planning and introduction of Voluntary Retirement scheme (without replacement) to reduce surplus manpower.
- Judicious mechanisation of various mining operation.
- Avoidance of wasteful expenditure.

Safety measures

With the continuous depletion of near surface ore deposits, mining is progressively being extended to deeper horizons and extraction is increasingly done through underground working which requires extra attention to be paid to various aspects such as, support system, ventilation and efficient filling of the voids arising out of extraction of ore. Continuous emphasis is laid on training of employees and mine working are regularly inspected by members of Pit Safety Committees, Workman Inspectors, Safety

Officer and G.M.(Safety).Safety weeks are observed and exhibitions are held to inculcate safety habits. Safety Committee meetings are regularly held during which any unsafe act committed /observed is discussed to avoid recurrence.

The Company pays special attention to ensure safety of the mines and work force employed therein. The Company has participated in Regional Safety Competition and won 18 prizes including the best overall prize in underground and Semi-Mechanised opencast.

Workers' participation in management

The Company has set up a mechanism for the association of workers representatives from the grass root level to the Apex Council which functions at the Corporate level, with workers and Management representatives under the chairmanship of the Chairman-cum-Managing Director to review and find solution to major problems, There is continuing effort to strengthen this arrangement. In addition, works/ Canteen/ Grievance committees are functioning satisfactorily at each unit. The members of these committees are from different sections of employees,

Environmental protection

The Company is conscious of its responsibility towards protection of environment in it's leasehold areas. 76,000 saplings were planted during 1997-98 at different mines with a survival rate of about 75%. The sericulture project at Gumgaon Mine has been further extended to make it commercially viable.

Progressive Use/Awards for Implementation of Hindi

In order to ensure progressive use of Hindi and implementation of Official Language Act, effective steps have been taken by the Hindi Cell, functioning at the Corporate Office of the company.

To encourage the use of Hindi at all levels various competitions are organised during "Hindi Fortnight" and the winners are suitably rewarded. Facilities for learning Hindi have been made available to employees who are not proficient in the language.

The Company has won second prize i.e. Indira Gandhi Raj Bhasha Award for 1996-97. The Company has also been awarded "Chal-Vyajayanti" prize by the Ministry of Steel for progressive use of Hindi and implementation of Official Language Act.

Social commitment

MOIL had adopted a Tribal village viz. Gondi, close to Ukwa Mine in Madhya Pradesh. The Company has introduced a wide range of development activities such as repair of roads, construction of houses for homeless tribals, construction of school building to impart education to tribal children etc. as a part of their ongoing to promote social welfare.

Personnel

The composition of the work force of the Company as on 1st October 1998 was as under:

Group	SC	ST	OBC	Others	Total
A	18	7	22	168	215
B	25	12	19	165	221
C	345	397	475	717	1934
D	1087	1629	2100	887	5703
Total	1475	2045	2616	1937	8073

Out of the total number of 8,073 employees 1,023 are

MSTC Limited

MSTC Limited was incorporated under the Companies Act, 1956 on 9th September, 1964 and was the Canalising Agent for import of carbon steel melting scrap, sponge iron/ hot briquetted iron and rerollable scrap till February, 1992. It was also the canalising agency for import of old ships for breaking, import of which was decanalised and put under OGL w.e.f. August, 1991. The Company also undertakes disposal of ferrous and non-ferrous scrap arisings from integrated steel plants under SAIL/RINL etc. and disposal of scrap, surplus stores, etc. from other Public Sector Undertakings and Govt. Departments.

Capital structure

The Company has an authorised capital of Rs.5 Crores and paid up capital of Rs.2.20 Crores as on 31.3.98 of which approximately 90% is held by President of India and balance 10% is held by Steel Furnaces Association of India, Iron and Steel Scrap Association of India and others.

Location of units

The Company's registered and corporate office is located at Calcutta and it has four Regional offices at Calcutta, Delhi, Chennai and Mumbai, four branch offices at Vizag, Bhopal, Bangalore and Vadodara and two resident offices at Bokaro and Rourkela.

Activities

The Company has two operational Divisions, i.e., International Marketing and Domestic Marketing.

This Division is responsible for disposal of ferrous scrap and other secondary arisings generated in public sector steel plants under SAIL and RINL as well as disposal of scrap, surplus stores, etc. from other public sector enterprises and Govt. Departments including Ministry of Defence.

This Division till February, 1992 largely undertook canalised import of carbon steel melting scrap, stainless steel, HBI/Sponge Iron, rerollable scrap, ships for breaking etc. for the secondary steel sector. After decanalisation, this Division no longer deals with any canalised item and arranges imports of scrap as well as other items as per the needs of actual users in competition with other private sector importers.

Organisational structure

The Chief Executive Officer of the Company is the Chairman-cum-Managing Director who is assisted by three Chief General Managers and five General Managers in-charge of various Divisions.

Marketing scenario: 1997-98

MSTC has been dealing with only one product, i.e., Carbon Steel Melting Scrap for the last few years. This business is dependent on fluctuations in the fortunes of Electric Arc Furnaces/ Induction Furnaces sector. Key determining factors for demand are international prices of scrap, freight market, foreign exchange conversion rate and domestic prices of finished product. Steel Industry continues to face slowing down of growth. Import of scrap by MSTC is for consumers in secondary steel sector. MSTCs bulk consumers in this sector are big units who are buying scrap themselves without depending on third party. These units are also diverting part of the supplies to small consumers. Since these units are using their own VABALs for import, MSTC finds it difficult to penetrate this sector.

Performance during 1997-98

In 1997-98, the total volume of business achieved was Rs.497 crores against a target of Rs.710 crores. Out of Rs.710 crores, Rs.210 crores was for International Marketing.

Due to reduced demand of scrap in the depressed market, most of the importers have had to sell their materials imported during 1996-97 and 1997-98 at a loss. MSTC also sold off their stock at loss due to depressed market condition. As a policy decision, MSTC did not venture into fresh imports till the existing stock was liquidated. In view of the above, it has not been possible to achieve FT target as no import was possible in absence of back to back 100% financial arrangement. International prices of scrap continue to fan and there was no growth of demand of imported scrap in the domestic market.

Against the target of Rs. 500 crores in domestic marketing achievement was Rs. 497 crores. Despite adverse domestic market conditions, the achievement was still 13% higher than 1996-97.

Strategy for 1998-99

For 1998-99 target of Rs. 565 crores has been fixed for domestic marketing and Rs.100 Crores for International Marketing which is about 13% more than the achievement of last year. Such growth can be achieved only if the market comes out of the present difficult phase and a period of growth starts. Achievement till September 1998 has been Rs.215.56 crores which is more than MOU target till date.

Due to low demand in ferrous scrap, MSTC has widened their import basket and imported Superior Kerosene Oil (SKO), furnace oil and slab end cuttings which are nontraditional items. The target in this sector was Rs.100 crores and it expects to achieve the same during 1998-99.

MOU with Government

Inspire of slow growth in the domestic market and instability in the prices of scrap in the international market, MSTC has been awarded "FAIR" rating by DPE on MOU Performance evaluation based on provisional figures of 1997-98. MSTC expects that MOU rating for 1998-99 will improve.

Ferro Scrap Nigam Limited

Ferro Scrap Nigam Limited (FSNL) is a joint sector company under the Ministry of Steel with a paid up capital of Rs.200 lakhs in which M/S MSTC holds 60% of the equity shares and the remaining 40% are held by M/S Harsco Inc.,of USA. The Company is thus a subsidiary of MSTC.

Activities and objectives

The Company undertakes the recovery and processing of scrap from slag and refuse dumps in the six steel plants at Rourkela, Burnpur, Bhilai, Bokaro, Visakhapatnam and Durgapur. The scrap recovered is returned to the steel plants for recycling/ disposal and the company is paid processing charges on the quantity recovered at varying rates depending on the category of scrap. Scrap is generated during Iron & Steel making and also in the Rolling Mills.

In addition, the Company is also providing Steel Mill services such as Scarfing of Slabs, handling of BOF Slag etc.

Organisational structure

The Chief Executive Officer of the Company is the Managing Director who normally functions under the guidance of a part time Chairman and a Board of Directors. The Managing Director is assisted by two General Managers and eight Deputy General Managers who are incharge of activities at the main steel plants, personnel and other functions at Corporate Office. The Corporate Office is situated at Bhilai and the Corporation has six field units in the steel plants at Bhilai, Burnpur, Rourkela, Bokaro, Visakhapatnam and Durgapur.

Physical and financial performance

The production performance of FSNL for the last two years and for the year 1998-99 (upto 30.09.98) are given below :

Item	1996-97	1997-98	1998-99 (Upto 30.9.98 (Prov.)
Recovery of scrap (Lakhs M.Ts)	13.03	14.73	6.82
Market Value of Production (Rs. in Crores)	573.32	648.11	300.08

Financial performance (Rs. in lakhs)

Item	1996-97	1997-98	1998-99 (Upto 30.9.98 (Prov.)
Total Turnover (i.e. service charges realised including misc. income etc.)	6497.12	7214.48	3390.91
Gross Margin before interest and depreciation	2354.15	238.94	1152.91
Interest and Depreciation	618.70	567.77	530.80
Profit before tax	1407.08	1817.16	622.09

Sales realisation:

Sales realisation permetric tonne for the last two years and for the year 1998-99 upto 30.09.98 are indicated below:

1996-97	1997-98	1998-99 (Upto 30.9.98 Prov.)
490.46	479.26	497.20

The Employment statistics of the company, including SC/ST as on 30.09.98, are given below

	Executive	Non-Executive	Total
Corporate Office	27	42	69
Rourkela Unit	20	204	224
Bhilai Unit	19	277	296
Burnpur Unit	15	123	138
Bokaro Unit	19	213	232
Vizag Unit	21	211	232
Durgapur Unit	17	138	155
Total	138	1208	1346

Future programmes

The integrated steel plants have switched over from conventional open hearth route to BOF-concast route. This has resulted in reduction in scrap arisings without affecting the demand for high quality scrap.

In order to meet the requirements of the integrated Steel Plants both in quality and quantity of scrap, FSNL is going for modernisation so as to upgrade the present technology for which discussion with Heckett MultiServ is in progress.

The new jobs undertaken by the company in 1997-98 are as follows:

- Scarfing of slabs at Bokaro Steel Plant
- Crushing, Screening and transportation of L. D. Slag to be used in the Sintering Plant, Blast Furnace and as Rail Ballast has been started at Rourkela, Durgapur and Vizag Person Steel Plants.

In addition, FSNL is also contemplating to expand their activities in the Private Sector Steel Plants for scrap recovery and processing jobs. In this connection, discussions have been held with M/s. ESSAR Steel Ltd.,

Jindal Vijaynagaram Steel Ltd and M/s. Neelachal Ispat Nigam Ltd., Bhubaneswar.

MOU with Government

The Company has been awarded 'Excellent' rating by DPE on MOU Performance evaluation for the year 199798. The Physical and Financial performance of the Company for the half year ending 30th September'98 is 108.08% & 103.05% respectively against the target as compared to 107.94% & 101.85% respectively for the same period during 1997-98.

Sponge Iron India Limited (SIIL)

Sponge Iron Plant of the Company was initially established as a demonstration unit with a capacity of 30,000 tpa with UNDP/UNIDO assistance to establish die technoeconomic feasibility of producing sponge iron (a part substitute for ferrous scrap used by steel-melting electric arc furnaces) from lump iron ore and 100% non-coking coal. The unit, based on non coking coal from Singareni Collieries Company Limited (SCCL) and iron ores available at various regions in Andhra Pradesh and neighbouring states of Madhya Pradesh and Karnataka went into regular operations in November, 1980. Being a Demonstration plant it is designed to be operated on a semi commercial basis, i.e. both for production of saleable product and for R&D work. Several improvement and modifications were effected to the Sponge Iron Plant based on Rotary Kiln Process to suit the local raw materials and operating conditions, as a result of which it has not only established the viability of the technology but also paved way for the development of Sponge Iron Industry in the Country.

Taking note of the successful operations of the Demonstration Plant, Government of India approved doubling its capacity from 30,000 tpa to 60,000 tpa by setting up a second kiln of like capacity. This unit, which was designed and bat by the Company's engineers incorporating various improvements and design modifications carried out in the Demonstration Plant for adapting the technology to Indian conditions, went into regular production from October, 1985.

The Company has also successfully designed and built a plant for briquetting of sponge iron fines (below 5 mm size) which were earlier not usable by electric arc furnaces and were being discarded. The Briquetting Plant was commissioned during October, 1987 and is operating to capacity.

A new and innovative project aimed at conservation of energy was commissioned with effect from 1.3.1993 for effectively utilising the sensible heat in the kiln off-gases for generation of electric power. By doing so it has not only improved the thermal efficiency of the process but also substantially reduced the dependence on external power thus effecting saving in costs. The Submerged Arc Furnace Project with an installed capacity of 45,000 tpa is set up by SIIL for smelting sponge iron (including sponge iron fines) into high quality (low phos,) pig iron. After having completed the trial runs by January, 1996 wherein it was established that the plant could achieve chemical composition at the required level for special grade pig iron, the plant was shutdown without going in for commercial operations due to Shortage of availability of power, unremunerative pricing and input cost escalation.

In order to utilise the existing infrastructure installed with a capital cost of about Rs.30 crores possibilities of going in for production of Ferro Alloys have been explored, during which it was found that production of Silico Manganese can be taken up with the existing furnace and other equipments after making some modifications. As per the current estimates the SAF

Plant would be taking up production of Silico Manganese. Necessary modifications have been carried out during the second half of 1997-98.

Finance

The authorised share capital of the Company stood at Rs.40.00 crores on 31/3/1998; paid up capital was Rs.32.58 crores. (Rs.31.75 crores held by Government of India and the balance of Rs.0.83 crore by the Government of Andhra Pradesh).

As against the target of 26,800 tonnes, actual sponge iron production upto Sept. 1998 was 24,574 tonnes representing 92% of the target.

Sales and profitability

Against a target of 34,300 tonnes upto 30 September, 1998, actual despatches were 29,545 tonnes representing 86% achievement of the target.

Operations upto the end of 30' September, 1998 have resulted in an provisional net loss of Rs.253 lakhs.

Cost reduction

Earlier iron ore size to feed in to rotary kiln was altered from 5-20mm to 3-20mm for improving the economics of operations. +20mm. size ore used to be crushed to obtain necessary size of 3-20mm for reduction plants. During curshing of ore less than 3mm size fines are generated and are considered as waste. They have to be disposed off at cheaper rates, In order to reduce the specific iron ore consumption as well as cost of production, it was planned to procure calibrated iron ore of size 5-15 mm from M/s National Mineral Development Corporation (NMDC), Bailadilla. After continuous follow up with NMDC, company succeeded in getting ore of required size (5 to 15mm). This allowed to feed ore as it is into rotary kiln for reduction by eliminating the ore preparation like oversize crushing, scrubbing, etc.

Efforts are made to procure sized limestone of 0 to 5mm instead of purchasing lumpy limestone and crushing the same to the required size. This reduced the cost of crushing and conveying and also the handling losses.

Control over purchase of equipment spares and consumables resulted in saving of about Rs.9,34,638/- when compared to previous year. Inventory level of spares and consumables was brought down from Rs.188.64 lakhs to Rs.171,00 lakhs. Savings in the consumption of raw materials have been effected by improving quality and by bringing down inventory level of principal raw materials i.e., iron ore and coal. By generating 22,59,800 units of power during the period from April, 1998 to September, 1998, there was a saving of Rs.26.26 lakhs worth of electrical energy otherwise to be drawn from State Electricity Board.

Efforts made towards indigenisation

The first reduction plant was set up by Lurgie Chemie of West Germany. Hence most of the equipment were imported from Germany. As a part of indigenisation about Rs.1.30 lakhs worth radiation protection tubes were procured locally for replacement of imported spares during the half year.

Employees participation in management

As per the directives of the Government of India, a Scheme for Employees participation in Management has been implemented in the Company. Various Committees under 'Workers' Participation in Management' have been reconstituted w.e.f. 25/7/1996. The Committees are functioning systematically and the contribution by way of suggestions made by the members so far have given reasonably good results which, in turn, resulted in improvement of overall performance of the plant. One

Plant level Committee, Works Committee, two Shop Level Committees, Canteen Management Committee, Safety Committee, Communal harmony Committee and Games and Sports Committee have been constituted with representatives of Management and the employees and regular meetings are held to discuss various problems and finding solutions internally. Members of the other registered Trade Unions were also included in various Committees. As directed by the Government of India and in order to increase induction of women at various levels in the Management, the women employees are also included in various statutory and non-statutory committees.

Hindi implementation

From 01/04/1998 to 30/9/1998, 70 documents were released in bilingual form in accordance with Section 3(3) of Official languages Act, 1963. 'Learn Hindi Sentences' Scheme is under progress. Hindi Day has been celebrated on 14/9/1998 and Essay Writing and Elocution Competitions were conducted and winners were rewarded with prizes.

Anti-Pollution measures

As a part of afforestation programme to control pollution levels, about 400 plants were planted. Regularly the pollution level of stacks emissions and water outlets are being checked by A.P. Pollution Control Board and the actions suggested by them, basing on their report, are attended immediately. Besides with available facilities pollution level monitoring is done departmentally also, to keep pollution levels within control.

Waste land development

About 2.5 hectors of waste land was levelled and about 360 saplings were planted as a part of afforestation and waste land development during the half year.

Metallurgical & Engineering Consultants (India) Ltd. (MECON)

As the first consultancy and engineering organisation in the country to be accredited with ISO:9001, the last 59 years have seen MECON emerging as one of the largest design, engineering and consultancy organisations in the world. It has developed considerable expertise not only in the field of consultancy services like design, basic & detailed engineering, front end engineering, project management, construction & site management services etc., but also in design and supply of equipment for the ferrous, non-ferrous, oil and gas, petrochemical and other general industries on engineering, procurement, construction & commissioning (EPCC) basis. This expertise has helped the company to bridge the knowledge gap in the country in high technology areas. MECON has diversified its services into power, environmental engineering, ocean engineering, ports & harbours, roads, highways & bridges, petro-chemicals, gas pipelines, material handling.

Long association with integrated steel plants has enabled MECON to build a strong technological base. The organisation has acquired, absorbed and innovated technologies to suit the needs of clients. It continues to acquire state-of-the-art technologies from developed countries like USA, France, Netherland, Switzerland, Germany, UK, Italy, China, Austria, etc. The know-how acquired has been successfully assimilated through direct on-the-job experience.

MECON has developed its own design for coke oven batteries and is one amongst the few in the world to have the know-how in this area. Today, coke oven batteries designed by MECON are operating at Durgapur and Rourkela Steel Plants. Towards further development in this direction, MECON, in collaboration with M/s GIPROKOKS, Russia has executed the first 7 meters tall coke oven battery in the country, at Bhilai in 1988. MECON has successfully executed design, erection, heating up and commissioning including guarantee test for 7 meters tall Coke Oven Batteries and Coke Dry Cooling Plants at Visakhapatnam Steel Plant, Bokaro Steel Plant, Bhilai Steel Plant, and other Private Sector Units.

In the field of Coal and Chemicals, MECON has designed and supplied 30,000 t/yr Benzol Plant based on state-of-the-art hydro refining process at Visakhapatnam Steel Plant. MECON has also executed, Acid re-generation plant on a turnkey basis for the Bokaro Steel Plant and Sulphuric Acid Plant for Bhilai steel Plant.

In the area of Continuous Casting MECON in association with M/s MDH of Germany has executed CCP - II Project, on turnkey basis, under Modernisation of Rourkela Steel Plant.

MECON has executed, on turnkey basis, converter Gas Cleaning Plant for Converters 1, 2 & 3 for Visakhapatnam Steel Plant.

In the area of Blast Furnaces, MECON has undertaken modernisation, technological upgradation services for Bhilai, Durgapur, IISCO, Burnpur, Rourkela and Bokaro Steel Plants. MECON is providing consultancy services for setting up Integrated Steel Plant for Neelachal Ispat Nigam Limited and Jindal Vijaynagar Steel Ltd. (based on Corex technology), etc.

In addition to Iron & Steel, MECON has rendered its services to various other sectors like Petro - chemical & refinery, power generation both captive & utility units, infrastructure development, bulk material facility, non-ferrous, raw material & mining, environmental engineering, etc. Some of the areas are detailed in subsequent paragraphs.

MECON has played a significant role in serving nonferrous industries. We are at present rendering our detailed engineering services for installation of Aluminium. Foil Plant of Hindalco at Silvasa, cold rolling mill complex of BALCO at Korba, aluminium automotive wheel project of Hindalco & NALCO and EPC services for upgradation of alumina plant of MALCO.

MECON is associated in setting up an external coal handling system on turnkey basis for TNEB for its North Chennai Thermal Power Project. MECON has also provided its services for handling of Iron ore and other raw materials as well.

MECON offers complete spectrum of consultancy & engineering services in the field of Environment. We have rendered our services to various projects funded by multilateral agencies Eke World Bank/ DFID/ OECF and other industries Eke SAIL, NFC, IREL, HCL, HZL, BALCO, FACOR, TISCO, etc. for various pollution control projects

In the field of Highway & transportation, MECON has carried out a number of assignments. At present we are rendering our services to Haldia Development Authority. MECON also carries out traffic & transportation study. At present Govt. of Maharashtra has asked us to provide services for two flyovers in Mumbai.

MECON occupies a strong place in rendering its expert engineering services in planning infrastructure water supply facilities, water treatment, water circulation systems.

Capital structure

As on 31.3.98 the authorised capital of the company was Rs. 400 lakhs. The issued subscribed and fully paid -up equity share capital was Rs. 241.84 lakhs of which Rs. 40.31 lakhs was on account of Bonus shares issued during 1996 - 97.

Major assignment domestic

- Detailed engineering & consultancy services for BOF complex of integrated steel plant at Satarda for Usha Ispat Ltd.
- Detailed engineering & consultancy services for sinter fines disposal system in sinter plant no. 3 of BSP.
- Study report for energy efficiency improvement in secondary steel sector for Govt. of India (Ministry of Steel)-
- Consultancy services for coke oven battery no. 1, 2 & 3 and CCD of VSP.

Rolling mill

- Detailed engineering, design & consultancy for hot & cold annealing & pickling line of Jindal Strips Ltd, Hissar.
- Design & Engineering for Modernisation and Supply of Equipment for existing 4 - Hi Cold Rolling Mill including Supervision of Erection & Commissioning for Vallabh Steels Limited, Ludhiana.
- Supply & installation of Optical Guide Setting Projector with Light Sources for Finishing Blocks of Wire Rod Mill for Visakhapatnam Steel Plant, Visakhapatnam.

Petro Chemical & Refinery

- Detailed engineering & consultancy services for mechanised Petro coke handling facilities at Barauni refinery of IOCL.
- Consultancy services for POL terminal of IOCL at Jasidih.
- Consultancy services for petroleum coke handling system of RPL at Jamnagar.

- Consultancy services for Koyali Pipeline Oil Terminal of IOCL.
- Consultancy services for Oil Accounting System of IOCL.

Power

- Detailed engineering & consultancy services for setting up a 25MW captive Power Plant for Usha Martine Infrastructure Services Ltd.
- Consultancy services for Refurbishment of Obra Thermal Power Station of UPSEB.
- Consultancy services for Balimela Hydro Electric Power Project in Orissa.
- Detailed engineering & consultancy services for CO boiler at HPCL, Vizag.

Non - Ferrous

- Detailed engineering & consultancy services for installation of aluminium alloy wheel plant for NALCO.
- Detailed engineering & consultancy services for expansion of Zinc smelter at Vizag, for HZL.
- Detailed engineering & consultancy services for expansion of Zinc smelter at Debari, for HZL.
- Engineering & consultancy services for aluminium toll project products for International Aluminium Products Limited.
- Consultancy services for Copper Cathod Granules Plant of Bhagyanagar Limited, Secunderabad.

Hydro Engineering

- Detailed engineering & consultancy service for pressurised water circulation systems Barauni Refinery of IOCL.

- Consultancy & project management services for water supply system for Haldia Development Authority.

Roads, Highways & Bridges

- Engineering & consultancy service for two flyovers of Maharastra State Road Development Corporation Ltd.
- Consultancy services for Kalghatgi—Dharwad Road for Nandi Highway Developers, Pune.

Bulk material handling

- Design, engineering, manufacture, supply, storage, construction of civil & structural works, erection, painting, testing & commissioning of External Coal Handling System - Package II for Tamil nadu Electricity Board, Chennai.
- Engineering & consultancy services for Material Handling Facilities at Vizag Port for NALCO.

8

Regulation and Conservation Indian Bureau of Mines

The Indian Bureau of Mines (IBM) is a subordinate organisation under the Department of Mines, Ministry of Steel and Mines. It is engaged in the promotion, conservation and scientific development of all the mineral resources of the country, other than coal, petroleum and natural gas, atomic minerals and minor minerals.

Towards this end it performs regulatory functions, namely enforcement of the Mines and Minerals (Regulation and Development) Act 1957, Mineral Concession Rules 1960 and Mineral Conservation and Development Rules 1988 and the relevant provisions of the Environmental Protection Act 1986. It also undertakes scientific, tech no-economic, research oriented studies in various aspects of mining, such as geological studies, ore beneficiation and environmental issues.

It provides Technical Consultancy services to the mining industry for the geological appraisal of mineral resources, and the preparation of feasibility reports of mining projects, including beneficiation plants. It prepares Mineral Maps and a countrywide inventory of mineral resources of leasehold and freehold areas. IBM also functions as the Data Bank of Mines and Minerals and publishes statistical periodicals. It also brings out technical publications/monographs on individual mineral commodities and bulletins of topical interest. It advises the Central and State Governments on all aspects of mineral industry, trade and legislation.

IBM imparts training to technical and non-technical officials of IBM and also persons from the mineral industry and other agencies in India and abroad.

Organisational set-up

The IBM is organised into four functional divisions, namely, (i) Mines Control and Conservation of Minerals (MCCM) Division, (ii) Ore Dressing and Technical Consultancy Division, (iii) Mineral Economics, Statistics, Research and Publication Division, and (iv) Planning and Co-ordination Division having two sub-divisions :

(a) Administration, Establishment matters (including training), accounts with all other administrative and financial matters; and

(b) Planning and Co-ordination.

IBM has its headquarters at Nagpur and twelve regional offices at Ajmer, Bangalore, Bhubaneswar, Calcutta, Chennai, Dehradun, Hyderabad, Jabalpur, Marvao (Goa), Nagpur, Ranchi and Udaipur and two sub-regional offices at Guwahati and Nellore.

The IBM has well equipped ore dressing laboratories and pilot plants at Nagpur. Ajmer and Bangalore.

Performance review

The performance of IBM in respect of its main activities during the period under review is indicated in Annexure-1. During the year 1998-99 (upto Nov., 1998), 1758 violations of Mineral Conservation and Development Rules (MCDR) 1988 were pointed out in respect of 721 mines and 498 violations were fully rectified. Forty one prosecutions were launched in various courts. Six cases were decided in favour of IBM and 28 cases were compounded.

Cumulative number of mining plans received by the IBM at various Regional Offices since its introduction upto the end of November, 1998 were 8583. Out of these, 6645 mining plans were approved, 937 rejected, 723 withdrawn by the parties and 148 were pending with the parties for modification with reference to the comments conveyed to them after scrutiny. 121 mining plans were under scrutiny with the IBM at various Regional/Zonal offices and 9 mining plans were pending with the Directorate of Mines

Safety for their comments. However, the status of disposal of mining plans during 1998-99 (upto Nov. 98) is given in Annexure-I separately.

Measures for abatement of pollution and environmental protection

The IBM continued its activity of educating the mine-owners about pollution control and environmental protection in mines by organising Mines Environment and Mineral Conservation (MEMC) Weeks. The celebration of MEMC Weeks in the regions of IBM has promoted environmental awareness in the mining industry. During 1998-99 (upto November, 1998) two such programmes were organised under the aegis of the Bangalore Regional Office.

The IBM approves the mining plans which constitute a basic pre-requisite for the grant/renewal of mining leases and for the existing mines. Environment Impact Assessment and Environment Management Plan are the integral parts of the mining plan through which adequate environmental protection during mining operations is ensured.

Preparationo of Mineral Maps

During the year 1998-99 (upto Nov., 1998) preparation/ updation of mineral maps of copper, lead and zinc in AP, Bihar, Gujarat, Karnataka, Orissa, Rajasthan and Sikkim covering about 14,000 hectare area alongwith corresponding forest overlays was in progress.

Mineral Beneficiation

Mineral beneficiation studies including mineralogical testing and chemical analysis is intimately related to both conservation and development of mineral resources. During the year 1998-99 (upto Nov., 1998), 51 ore dressing investigations, 45,537 chemical analyses and 1,713 mineralogical examinations were completed. Besides, 7 in-plant studies were carried out during the period.

The task of compelling a compendium of R&D facilities for processing of ores/minerals over the years since India's independence, was entrusted to IBM by the Ministry. Accordingly, a compendium entitled "R&D Facilities for processing of Ores/Minerals in India" was prepared in IBM and was released by the Hon'ble Minister for Steel & Mines, Shri Naveen Patnaik.

Inventory of mineral resources and market survey report

Computerisation of National Mineral Inventory (NMI) updated as on 1.4.97 was completed for 4 minerals and analytical reviews of NMI as on 1.4.1995 were prepared for 13 minerals. Besides, a Handbook of NMI as on 1.4.95 was under preparation.

Market Survey study on China clay was in progress and a bulletin of Rare alloy metals in India was under printing.

A handbook on Non-ferrous Metals in India 199596 issue was released and annual bulletin on Consumption of Non-ferrous Metals in India, copper-lead-zinc, April 1997 - March 1998 issue was under printing. Besides, 2 quarterly reports on End-use metal consumption for copper, lead and zinc for quarters ending March 98 and June 98 were prepared.

Stastical publications

IBM disseminates statistical information on mines, minerals, metals and mineral based industries through its various publications. Information on mineral production, stocks, despatches, employment, inputs in mining, mining machinery and related matters received from the mine owners on statutory basis under the MCDR, 1998 and ancillary statistics on metals production, mineral trade and market prices of minerals, revenue from the mining sector, rent, royalty and cess on minerals, etc. from other agencies is compiled regularly by IBM.

The statistical publications released during the year 1998-99 (upto Nov., 1998) include Statistical Profile of Minerals, "1997-98 issue, Indian Mineral Industry at a Glance, 1996-97 issue and 7 issues (upto June, 1998) of Monthly Statistics of Mineral Production.

Concultancy service

IBM provides technical consultancy services on prescribed charges for geological appraisals, survey of the areas, preparation of feasibility study reports, environment impact assessment and environment management plan, selection of suitable mining equipment, evaluation of feasibility reports prepared by other consultants, financial institutions, etc. The assignments completed during the year 1998-99 (upto Nov., 1998) include (i) Collection of samples for chemical analysis from Ametha Limestone Mine for M/s N.M. Dubash Stone and Lime Co. and (ii) Coal stock measurement at various collieries of Coal India Ltd.

Besides, 5 assignments on preparation of Mining scheme/Preliminary Geological Appraisal reports were in progress.

Technical publications

IBM brings out technical publications relating to mines and minerals, mineral based industries, trade, beneficiation, R&D activities, etc. During the year 1998-99 (upto Nov., 1998), Volume-II of the Indian Minerals Year Book (IMYB), 1996 issue and Volumed of the IMYB, 1997 issue were released and Volume-II of the IMYB, 1997 issue was under printing. Besides, Directory of Mineral Consumers in India a bulletin on Mineral Royalties and 2 issues of half-yearly bulletin on Mineral Information (April-Sept., 97 and Oct., 97-March, 98) were released.

10.2 Under the series 'Mineral Facts and Problems' the Monograph on copper was under printing and preparation of Monograph on clay was in progress. A bulletin on Status of the Mining Industry based on special study reports (South Zone) was released.

11. Mining Research

11.1 Applied Mining Research is carried out on various mining aspects so as to help in systematic development of mines and improvement in productivity in mines through evolution of suitable norms. Industry sponsored assignments on environment and rock mechanics aspects on charge basis are also undertaken. During the period under review,* 2 assignments on preparation of EIA/EMP of Mokhana Limestone Mine for M/s Tata Chemicals Ltd. and Geotechnical investigation of Bhotang Copper Mine for M/s Sikkim Mining Corporation Ltd. were completed and report submitted to the parties. Besides, 5 assignments sponsored by the Industry on charge basis are in progress.

Training

IBM imparts training to technical and nontechnical officials of IBM and also to persons from mineral industry and other agencies in India and abroad. During the year 1998-99 (upto Nov., 1998) 17 training programmes were conducted in which a total of 109 IBM personnel and 68 industry personnel including 2 from North-Eastern states participated. Besides, under the MoU for co-operation between India and Vietnam in the field of Geology and Mineral Resources. IBM imparted training for one month to 3 Vietnamese Mining Engineers/Geologists.

Advising central and state governments on matters connected with the mining and mineral industry

IBM continued to advise the Central and State Governments on matters concerning mines and minerals, export and import policies, mineral consumption and industrial utilisation, recovery of by products, demand and supply of minerals, renewal of mining leases. Necessary material was also furnished to the Ministry for answering Parliament Questions during its various sessions. Assistance was also rendered to private parties, institutions and foreign organisations on subjects like mineral production, consumption and other statistics.

IBM Advisory board

The 11th meeting of the IBM Advisory Board was held on 3rd April 1998 at Nagpur under the Chairmanship of Shri B.B. Tandon, the then Secretary (Mines). During the meeting following important decisions/suggestions were made:

i) IBM should reduce its role as a regulatory body and increase its role as a facilitator even though both these functions are being performed by IBM commendably

ii) IBM to ensure total transparency and promptness in discharge of its duties.

iii) IBM should try to reduce the time taken for approving the mining plans and accord priority to this work and to maintain total transparency in the process.

iv) IBM should try to reduce the time lag between the preparation and release of various technical publications and also review the cost of the publications brought out by IBM.

v) The important investigations being undertaken by OD Laboratory of IBM should be patented.

vi) IBM and National Institute of Rock Mechanics, KGF, can collaborate together undertake Various projects on geotechnical studies, slope stability, etc.

Sub-committee to make recommendations to IBM advisoryr board for more effective functioning of IBM

The sub-committee constituted by the Department of Mines, Ministry of Steel and Mines to make recommendations to the IBM Advisory Board for effective functioning of IBM, submitted its modified report after deliberations in the meetings held on 29.4.98 and 24.9.98 to the Chairperson for further consideration.

Working group meetings

Indo-french working group

Shri A.N. Bose, Controller General, IBM visited France from 3-10 Oct., 1998 as a member of the Indian delegation for the 12th meeting of the Indo-French Working Group on Mineral Exploration and Development. During 4-6 Oct., 98 he visited BRGM Laboratories and attended the Expert Group Meeting at Orleans. He also attended the 12th meeting of the Indo-French Working Group on

Mineral Exploration and Development co-chaired by Shri B.B. Tandon, the then Secretary (Mines) on the 7th and the ceremony of signing of the protocol on the 8th Oct., 98 at Paris.

Indo-South African working group

As a member of the Indian delegation led by Shri B.B. Tandon, the then Secretary (Mines), Shri K.S. Raju, Director (OD) from IBM attended the first meeting of the Indo-South African Working Group on Geology and Mineral Resources from 13-19 August, 1998. At the end of the Working Group Meeting, a protocol was signed between India and South Africa. A total of 6 projects were identified for cooperation of which one project entitled 'Characterisation and processing of gold, diamond and platinum group metal/ ores' is to be in collaboration between IBM and one of the R&D laboratories in South Africa.

IBM-BRGM projects

Assistance for setting up of a Mineral Resource and Intelligence System (MRIS) Database at IBM, Nagpur:

Under the IBM-BRGM-MRIS Project, during the year 1998-99 (upto November, 98) Mines-cum-Production and Integration outputs were modified and installed at IBM, Nagpur. With this, all the databases namely National Mineral Inventory & Beneficiation (NMI&B), Mines cum Production (MCP), World Mineral Intelligence (WMI), External Trade & Mineral Consumption (ETMC) and Mining lease, Mining Permit Geological Information System (MLMP-GIS) and their screen out-puts have been installed by BRGM experts in the VAX/VMS 3100 server in IBM. The Termination Agreement of the IBM-BRGM-MRIS Project was signed on 9.11.98 at Nagpur between IBM and BRGM, France.

Project on Development of Application Techniques in relation to Environmental Management of Mines and Waste Recoveries:

Under this project, field studies were taken up in 1997-98 by IBM teams in 3 Mines Study Sites namely in North Goa and Sukinda in Orissa State for assessing regional environment impact and for preparation of Environmental Management Plan. In Rampura Agucha lead-zinc mine in Rajasthan processing and waste recovery was continued during the period under review, Baseline data generation and processing of data in respect of air quality, water quality and quantity, collection of soil sediments and aquatic life, dust gauge samples, noise level etc. for winter and summer seasons were completed and water quality and quantity monitoring in monsoon season was completed for North Goa and Sukinda Mines Study Sites.

Five BRGM experts visited IBM from 4-18 May 1998 on a mission to observe and guide the field work of IBM teams.

BRGM experts on Rock-Mechanics Study and Rehabilitation of Waste dumps visited IBM in November, '98. After the field visits to Goa and Sukinda Mines Study Sites, the sites for drilling boreholes for installation of piezo-meters for carrying out geotechnical study and also the parameters to be analysed for soil quality testing in connection with rehabilitation of waste dumps were finalised.

Technical management information system (TMIS)

An agreement between IBM and BRGM, France on 'Setting up of Technical Management Information System (TMIS) at IBM, Nagpur' at a cost of FRIF 23.4 million was signed on 22.6.98. The kick-off meeting of the project was held on 9.11.98 between BRGM experts and IBM counterparts at Nagpur and the project formally took off. As a Phase I activity the meetings between IBM and BRGM experts were held during 10-16 November, '98 for evaluation of the database general design and the draft report was signed.

BRGM experts alongwith IBM officers visited each Regional/Zonal office of IBM and had an on-the-spot assessment for installation of Computer System and the existing system of each proposed project site.

Software Training Programme on ORACLE 8.0 in WINDOW NT operating system for 38 officers/ staff of IBM was arranged at Nagpur in 3 batches.

Golden Jubilee celebration of IBM

On 1st March, 1998, IBM completed 50 years of its dedicated service to the Nation in particular to the Mineral Industry and is celebrating the Golden Jubilee Year. Special lectures by eminent Earth Scientists and other authorities were arranged at the IBM Headquarters, Nagpur and at the Regional Offices. A 3 days function was organised at Regional Ore Dressing Laboratory, Ajmer during 11-13 August, 1998. The Ore Dressing Laboratory and Pilot Plant were kept open to the public and to the students from educational institutions and universities to acquaint themselves with IBM's activities.

Mega event to commemorate the 50th anniversary of India's independence

Department of Mines, Ministry of Steel & Mines constituted an organising Committee to celebrate the Mega Event to commemorate the 50th anniversary of India's Independence, with Shri A.N. Bose, Controller General, IBM as its Chairman and Shri Satish Chander, Director (Mines) as Co-Chairman with CMDs of Public Sector Undertakings under the Department of Mines,

Secretary General, FIMI and Chief Executives of some of the reputed Business Houses as members.

To mark the momentous milestone of 50 years of India's Independence, the 'Mega Event' was celebrated from 6-8 August, 1998 at Nagpur. It was inaugurated by Shri Naveen Patnaik, Hon'ble Minister of Steel & Mines on 6th August, 1998. During the inauguration, the Hon'ble Minister released a Souvenir which contained the brief activities and functions of the Organisations and Public Sector Units under the Department of Mines and some important mining organisations. The Hon'ble Minister presented Special Awards to 15 Geo-scientists and Technologists for their distinguished contribution to the Mining Industry. A video presentation on 'Strides of Mineral Industry since Independence' was also arranged. The inauguration was followed by a Technical Seminar with its theme as 'Indian Mining Industry : A Perspective'. The Technical Seminar was spread over 5 technical sessions on these three days. Eminent Geo-scientists and Technologists from various organisations/mining industry of the country presented papers in these technical sessions. A compendium of all the 30 technical papers presented in the seminar was brought out on the occasion.

The valedictory function was held on 8.8.98 in which Shri Ramesh Bais, Hon'ble Minister of State for Steel & Mines was the Chief Guest and Shri Nitin Gadkari, Hon'ble Minister for Public Works and Guardian Minister for Nagpur, Government of Maharashtra was the Chairman. Shri R.K. Sharma, Secretary General, FIMI, New Delhi, gave a presentation of overview of the proceedings of the Technical Seminar. About 300 delegates from various - Organisations/Mining Industry participated in the Mega Event. An Exhibition was also arranged at Hotel Tuli International, Nagpur in which

IBM, GSI, MECL, BALCO, NALCO, HCL, HZL, BGML & JNARDDC participated.

Revenue generation in IBM

Revenue generated during 1998-99 (upto November, 1998) from the consultancy work in mining, geology, ore dressing and mining research work, training and through sale of publications etc. was Rs. 24.70 lakhs.

Foreiggn seminars/symposiums, etc.

Shri M.N. Makode, Suptdg. Officer (OD), IBM was deputed to China during 21-30 June, 1998 to witness the test work conducted by Beijing General Research Institute of Mining and Metallurgy (BGRIMM) and to study the reproducibility of the flowsheet developed by BGRIMM in connection with establishing a fluorite beneficiation plant for producing acid grade concentrates by the ESSEL Mining Industries, New Delhi.

Dr. (Mrs.) M.N. Gaikwad, Assistant Ore Dressing Officer, IBM participated in the Mineral Engineering Conference 1998 organised by Camborne School of Mines, University of Exeter (UK) during 14-16 September, 1998 at Edinburgh, Scotland and presented her research paper entitled 'Frother Blends - Effect on Flotation of Mixed Sulphide Ore of Malanjkhand Copper Project, Balaghat (India).

Computerisation

Local Area Network (LAN) has already been installed at IBM Headquarters Complex. The work on Wide Area Network (WAN) is also in progress. Regional/ Zonal Offices located at various cities are being connected with NIC district centres through dial-up modems for E-mail communications. Facility of internet surfing is also available in IBM.

Data Acquisition System (DAS) has been established and is in operation in the Pilot Plant of IBM. The DAS is used while conducting pilot plant test runs for controlling some of the circuits like pulp density in grinding circuits, pH in the flotation circuit, etc. and acquiring real time data from various field instruments like power consumption in Jaw crusher, Cone crusher, Ball mills, etc., pulp density and mass flow, water flow, pH values, temperatures etc. Off line data can also be entered in the system through manual data entry for storing and utilising in the report preparation.

Work done concerning women (perspective plan for women)

Indian Bureau of Mines has not drawn up any specific perspective plan for women, however, out of a total strength of employees, women employees constitute about 11 percent. Training was imparted to some women employees in the field of technical as well as administrative matters.

Women employees are also actively participating in various cultural and extra-curricular activities organised by IBM from time to time. The 'Women's Day' was observed during the National Integration Week.

Employment of SC/ST women as on 30.12.1998

Class	*Total No. of employees in position*	*No. of SC*	*No. of ST*	*No of Women*
Group A	245	50	19	8
Group B	88	11	5	6
Group B (NG)	55	7	6	13
Group C (Tech)	485	80	37	30
Group C (Min)	363	85	29	92
Group D	359	107	35	29
Total	1595	320	131	178

9

Overview of Aluminium, Zinc, Lead and Copper

A Perspective of aluminium

India has large resources of high grade bauxite deposits of the order of 3037 million tonnes (MT) (proved + probable + possible). The recoverable reserves are placed at 2525 MT. The proved and probable reserves are 1218 MT, placing the country fifth in rank in the world, next only to Australia, Guinea, Brazil and Jamaica. Even at an anticipated consumption of 7 million tonnes per annum of bauxite, these reserves are expected to last for over 350 years. Given the natural resource endowment, growing demand for aluminium and its alloys, economic opportunities and scope for exports, India can produce alumina at internationally competitive prices. Aluminium metal can also be produced competitively with the latest technology coupled with cheaper energy arrangements in India or by toll smelting alumina in low power cost aluminium smelters abroad. The greatest scope for value addition and employment lies in the development of downstream aluminium end-products like extrusions, rolled products, fabrications and finished items. India can benefit by this value addition given the low energy requirements and labour intensity of the downstream industries. Aluminium has significant industrial and economic importance for India as this is the one metal for which the country has abundant raw material. While our bauxite reserves account for 7.5% of the world's total deposits, our aluminium capacity is only 3% indicating the scope and need for new capacities to meet growing internal demand and for sizeable exports on a long term basis. Demand for aluminium is expected to grow rapidly with increasing use in the construction, power transmission, transport and packaging sectors. It may be noted that due to the poor natural resource endowment of other non-ferrous metals like copper, lead zinc, tin etc., where the country is heavily dependent on imports, aluminium and value added exports could help in the overall export-import balance of non-ferrous metals,

Bauxite

Alumina is produced from bauxite ore. About 1 tonne of alumina is produced from 3 tonnes of bauxite and about 1 tonne aluminium is produced from 2 tonnes of alumina.

About 89% of the recoverable reserves of bauxite are of metallurgical grades. Orissa, Andhra Pradesh, Madhya Pradesh, Gujarat, Maharashtra and Bihar are the principal states where bauxite deposits are located in India. Major bauxite reserves are concentrated in the East Coast bauxite deposits of Orissa and Andhra Pradesh.

Alumina

Aluminium metal is extracted from alumina in a smelter plant. For making one tonne of aluminium, roughly 2 tonnes of alumina is required. However, the power consumption for production of one tonne of aluminium is as high as 17500 KW per tonne of metal in India.

Aluminium

Aluminium is produced from alumina through smelting process. It has a variety of applications such as, in power transmission and distribution, manufacture of aircraft, spacecraft, kitchenware, architectural fittings, grain silos, industrial explosives, automobiles, etc. and also in defence sector.

The annual installed capacity for production of alumina in the country is as under :-

Unit in Tonnes,

Company	*Quantity*	*Location*	
NALCO	800,000*	Damanjodi	(Orissa)
BALCO	200,000	Korba	(Madhya Pradesh)
INDAL	312,000	Muri	(Bihar : 72,000)
		Belgaum	(Karnataka : 240,000)
HINDALCO	350,000	Renukoot	(Uttar Pradesh)
MALCO	50,000	Madras	(Tamil Nadu)

* Govt. has approved the expansion of the capacity of the bauxite mines from 2.4 million tonnes per year (MTPY) to 4.8 MTPY and that of the alumina refinery from 0.8 MTPY to 1.575 MTPY. Currently, the project is under implementation by NALCO and is progressing on schedule.

There are seven smelters with a total installed capacity of 714,000 TPY. Two plants with a total capacity of 330,000 TPY belonging to NALCO and BALCO are in public sector; five are in private sector. INDAL has three smelters operating at Allupuram, Hirakund and Belgaurn which are supported by alumina plants at Muri in Bihar and Belgaum in Karnataka.

Installed capacity of aluminium

Aluminium production in India commenced in 1943 with a modest 25,000 tonnes per annum capacity which grew to an installed capacity of 714,000 TPA. The five primary producers of aluminium metal in the country are given below :-

Public Sector	*Installed*	*Capacity*
NALCO	230,000	TPA*
BALCO	100,000	TPA
Private Sector		
HINDALCO	242,000	TPA
INDAL	1177,000	TPA
MALCO	25,000	TPA
Total	714000	TPA

Production of aluminium

.1 Production of aluminium by the primary producers in the country during the last five years is given below:

(In tonnes)

Name	*1994-95*	*1995-96*	*1996-97*	*1997-98*	*1998-99***
NALCO	178072	192288	203823	200162	99523
BALCO	92089	91240	91996	88198	67721
HINDALCO	164280	175398	164558	200304	178377
INDAL	47541	54084	37370	38823	31461
MALCO	–	16254*	22865	25853	19530
TOTAL	477801	529264	520612	553340	396612

* Smelter of MALCO was recommissioned during 1995-96. - Provisional figures upto December, 1998.

Exports of aluminium

The quantity of aluminium and its secondary products exported by the primary producers during the last five years is indicated below:-

(In tonnes)

Name	*1993-94*	*1994-95*	*1995-96*	*1996-97*	*1997-98*	*1998-99*
NALCO	52724	65309	49127	60357	55475	18231
BALCO	28	36	247	5324	NIL	NIL

(Contd..)

HIND-ALCO	9137	13236	16287	27352	26207	15057.401
INDAL	9525	11040	7739	NIL	NIL	497

Demand and consumption of alluminium by the domestic industry

India has been dependent upon imports of aluminium metal till 1988. With the commissioning of NALCO's plant in 1988 a sea change took place and the country which was net importer of aluminium became self-sufficient. Consequently, the Aluminium Control Order which regulated supplies and prices of indigenous aluminium was withdrawn on 1.3.1989. The table below indicates the production, demand, domestic consumption, exports and import of the metal from 1993-94 upto 1997-98:-

Year	*Production*	*Domesttic Consumption*	*Exports*	*Imports*
1993-94	465165	410000	89661	73994
1994-95	477801	353250	95099	109905
1995-96	529264	–	69636	125049
1996-97	520180	573000	86684	158744
1997-98	553340	–	523686*	82751*

(Export and import figures are based on the information given by DGCIS, Calcutta). *Upto January, 1998.

Steps taken by Govt. to improve availability of aluminium

To facilitate better availability of the metal in the country, the Govt. of India has permitted free import of aluminium under OGL.

(i) Excise duty on aluminium and its product is 15%.

(ii) Custom duty is applicable @ 20% ad-valorem. In addition, following decisions have been taken to increase production of aluminium in the country on a long term basis.

(iii) Exemption of aluminium metal and its down stream products from the provisions of compulsory licensing.

(iv) Reduction of excise duty on the metal and extension of MODVAT benefits to the aluminium industry.

(v) Inclusion of aluminium industry in the list of industries where automatic approval of foreign equity upto 51 % is available to encourage foreign investment in the sector.

The excise duty on the metal and its products ranging from 29% to 40% was reduced to uniform rate of 25% during 1993 Budget. This duty was further reduced to 20% during 1994 Budget and to 15% in 1995 Budget. Also, MODVAT has been extended to the aluminium industry including petroleum based raw material like CPC and Coal Tar Pitch used in the manufacture of aluminium.

ZINC

Zinc has been known since ancient times and has served mankind long before it was identified as a separate metal. About 50% of zinc produced worldwide is used for protective function. It is ranked fourth among metals in terms of consumption after Iron, Aluminium and Copper. About 7 million tonnes of zinc is consumed worldwide every year. Zinc has major applications in the galvanising industry and the battery sector. The current production capacity in India is 1,82,000 tonnes per annum in the primary sector and about 50,000 tonnes per annum in the secondary sector. It is estimated that during 1998-99 the zinc production in India would be about 1,64,000 tonnes in the primary sector.

The sectoral consumption of zinc in India is as follows : Galvanising (70%), Battery (10%), Zinc Alloys

(10%), Die-casting (5%), Chemicals and miscellaneous others (5%).

Lead

Among the non-ferrous metals, the consumption of lead ranks fourth after Aluminium, Copper and Zinc. The inertness and corrosion resistance, softness and ease of working with lead, are the principal reasons for its wide application.

Centuries old lead roofs are still sound. Its low melting point makes lead easy, both to cast and recover by remelting. It lends itself to alloying with other metals, including Antimony, Bismuth, Cadmium, Silver, and Tin. Softness of lead and its ability to alloy with other metals permit it to be rolled into sheets for chemical plants, corrosion resistant laboratory working surfaces, roofing damp-proof courses and ornamental work and to be extruded into rods, pipes and collapsible tubes. Other non-dissipative uses are in sound proofing and in radiation shielding for radiography in nuclear power. In tonnage terms, the principal modern uses of lead are in Lead-acid batteries, sheet and pipe, and glass. Battery manufacture is by far the largest single end-use for lead, accounting for an estimated 60% of consumption worldwide. The current lead production capacity in India is 89,000 tonnes per annum in the primary sector.

It is estimated that Lead production in India would be about 46,900 tonnes in the primary sector during 1998-99.

The main constraint in lead production in the country is the lack of lead ore reserves, which necessitates large scale imports and recycling. The sectoral consumption of lead is : Lead acid batteries (75%), Chemicals, Alloys/Pigment and others (20%), Cable Sheathing (5%).

Zinc and lead scenario in India

The identified zinc and lead resources in the country are estimated at 383 million tonnes. Out of this, 167 million tonnes containing 2.17% lead and 8.16% zinc fall under the category of mineable reserves. The bulk of the Lead-Zinc deposits occur in Rajasthan and are under lease/ exploitation of Hindustan Zinc Limited. A major multi-metal world-class deposit of zinc, lead and associated metals had been discovered in the Rampura-Agucha belt in Bhilwara district of Rajasthan, which has estimated ore reserves of 60.35 million tonnes containing 13.48% zinc and 1.93% lead. 12.2 The per capita annual consumption in India is 0.2 kg for zinc and 0.1 kg for lead. This is amongst the lowest in the developing world. The leading nation in consumption is the USA with 3.67 kgs of zinc and 5.14 kgs of lead being the annual per capita consumption. It is expected that the annual per capita consumption in India will go up to 281 grams of zinc and 170 grams of lead by the turn of this century.

Installed capacities

The present smelting capacity for zinc and lead metals in the country is 1,82,000 MT and 89,000 MT per annum respectively. The break-up of these capacities is indicated below:

(Unit: MT per annum)

Company	*Zinc*	*Lead*
Hindustan Zinc Limited (HZL)	152000	65000
Binani Industries Ltd. (BIL)	30000	–
Indian Lead Ltd. (ILL)	–	24000
Total	1,82,000	89,000

The break-up of production capacities of individual units of HZIL is as under:

Name of the Smelter	*Zinc*	*Lead*
Debari (Rajasthan)	49000	–
Vizag (Andhra Pradesh)	33000	22000
Chanderiya (Rajasthan)	70000	35000
Tundoo (Bihar)	–	8000
Total	152000	65000

While HZL is a Public Sector Undertaking, BIL and ILL are in the private sector. BIL produces zinc from imported concentrates at the Alwaye (Kerala) Plant. ILL has two units at Calcutta and Thane (Maharashtra) having 12000 MT per annum capacity each. Both units are based on imported concentrates/ scraps. Besides these units, both zinc and lead are also produced through the secondary routes from scrap, dross, residue, etc. Most of the secondary producing units, especially in lead, are in the unorganised sector.

Production vis-a-vis demand

SThe table below indicates the details of demand and production for zinc and lead during the last five years:

(in MTS.)

	Zinc			*Lead*		
Year	*Demand*	*Prodn.*	*Gap*	*Demand*	*Prodn.*	*Gap*
1994-95	191800	149213	42587	75300	49274	26026
1995-96	201600	141374	60226	80100	45655	34445
1996-97	215900	140000	75900	84000	43780	40220
1997-98	224000	165000	59000	87400	44604	42796
1998-99	240100	164000	76100	98100	46900	51200
	(estimated)			(estimated)		

The gap between indigenous production and demand is met through recycling of secondaries like scrap, dross, residues, etc. and import under OGL. The demand for zinc and lead has grown at an annual rate of approximately 4% and 5% respectively, during the 8th Five Year Plan. With the projected high growth in the 9th Plan and particularly, of Steel Industry (and demand for galvanisation with Zinc) and automobile industry (with automotive batteries with lead as major input), the demand for Lead and Zinc in India is expected to grow rapidly during the 9th Five Year Plan period. As per the Working Group Report for the 9th Plan, Zinc demand is expected to grow at the rate of 4.5 to 6.0% and for Lead at the rate of 5 to 7% during the 9th Plan.

Copper survey

The present copper ore resources of the country are estimated at 730 million tonnes averaging 1.17% metal content. Out of this 4.30 million tonnes of ore with an average grade of 1.21 % copper is under mining lease held by Hindustan Copper Limited.

The other important small Mining Units are operated by Sikkim Mining Corporation (SMC) at Rangpo, Sikkim and Hutti Gold Mines Ltd. (HGML) at Chitradurga and Kalyani in Karnataka.

Hindustan Copper Ltd (HCL) is the sole producer of primary copper in the country. The total installed capacity of HCL is 47,500 tpa. Besides this, HCL has a continuous Cast Copper Wire Rod Plant at Taloja to produce 60,000 tpa Wire Rods.

The per capita consumption of refined copper metal in India is 0.30 Kg which is very low against world average per capita consumption of 3 Kg and per capita consumption of more than 10 Kg in advanced countries. 15.5 The New Industrial Policy announced by the Government in July, 1991 inter alia envisages that no Industrial Licence is required for production of copper in the country.

In the wake of the liberalisation policy of the Govt. a number of smelters have been set up in the private sector. The existing smelter capacities are tabulated below:

(in TPA)

	Existing capacity
Hindustan Copper Ltd.	47,500
Sterlite Copper Co.	60,000
Birla Copper	100,000
SWIL Ltd.	50,000*
Total :	257,000

*Likely to be commissioned soon

While there has been five-fold increase in smelting capacity in the last three years, there has been no corresponding increase in indigenous production of copper concentrates. Therefore, the total increased capacity of smelters is based on import of copper concentrates.

10

Mining and Processing

National aluminium company limited

National Aluminium Company Limited (NALCO) was incorporated on 7th January 1981 as a wholly owned Government company to exploit a part of the large deposits of bauxite discovered in the East Coast. Aluminium Pechiney of France, a world leader in the field, provided the technology and basic engineering for bauxite mining, alumina refinery and smelter. The project cost of Rs. 2408 crore was partly financed by Rs. 1119 crore equivalent of Euro-Dollar loans extended by a consortium of international banks and the balance Rs. 1289 crore through equity from Government of India.

Under extremely difficult logistics of implementing a multi-locational greenfield project, NALCO successfully constructed and commissioned each of its units on schedule and within estimated cost, a feat which has few parallels in the annals of Indian Public Sector history. NALCO's various production units, their locations and installed capacities are :

◆ Bauxite Mines	Panchpatmalli	22,400,000	TPY
◆ Alumina Refinery	Damanjodi	800,000	TPY
◆ Smkelter Plant	Angul	230,000	TPY
◆ Captive Power Plant	Angul	720	MW
◆ Port Facilities	Vizag	375,000	TPY

The Commissioning dates of the various facilities a as follows :

- Port facilities – September, 1985
- Bauxite Mines – November, 1985
- Alumina Refinery – September, 1986
- Captive Power Plant – September, 1986
- Smelter – March, 1987

.3 The systems support for the complex includes a coal mine and coal handling plant set up by the Mahanadi Coalfields Limited.

The Company is managed by a Board of Directors headed by the Chairman-cum-Managing Director and assisted by whole time functional Directors in the areas of Projects & Technical, Finance, Production and Personnel & Administration.

Physical performance

The production of NALCO during the year 1997-98 and 1998-99 are given below :

(Figure in Tonnes)

Items	*Unit*	*95-96*	*96-97*	*97-98*	*Target for 98-99 Dec./'98*	*1998-99 Actuals Upto 98-99)*	*Annual estimate (RE*
Bauxite (Crushed & Transported	'000MT	2408	2558	2662	2550	1808.69	2700
Calcined Alumina	'000MT	807	840	883	850	654.60	897.5
Aluminium	'000MT	192	204	200	218	99.52	150
Net Power Generation of CPP	MU	4147	4187	3902	4100	2590.02	3950

Financial performance

Operating results

Details	*95-96 Actuals*	*96-97 Actuals*	*97-98 Actuals*	*Annual Target 98-99 (BE)*	*Actual upto Dec '98*	*Annual esti-mates 98-99 (RE)*
Income	1813.05	1818.70	1983.71	2093.81	1194.47	1848.24
Operating cost	927.17	987.89	1052.71	1120.90	723.38	1056.99
Interest etc.	64.83	9.08	33.57	16.56	32.75	32.775
Depreciation and amortisation	285.78	265.82	272.00	281.95	205.78	278.74
Net Profit before tax and dividend	535.27	555.91	625.43	674.40	232.56	479.76

Aluminium smelter crisis

During the year 1998, NALCO had to shut down the operation of a number of pots in its Smelter plant at Angul, Orissa. In view of the gravity of the problem, Government ordered an Enquiry Committee to look into the problems affecting the smelter of NALCO and consequent loss of production. The Committee was constituted on 12.6.1998 under the chairmanship of Dr. C.G. Krishnadas Nair, Chairman , HAL.

The Enquiry Committee submitted its report on 4th August 1998. The Committee has broadly come to the conclusion that the gradual deterioration in the performance of pots over the years is mainly due to non-adherence to the standard operating practices, improper maintenance, poor work culture, improper planning and lack of team work. The Committee made several recommendations to avoid recurrence of such failure in future. The Company has taken action on the recommendations of the Enquiry Committee and the position has improved. The number of pots, which had touched the level of 239 pots on 22.7.98, has since improved to 367 pots as on 3.1.1999. The quality of the metal produced has also improved and export of metal has been resumed.

Sales performance

Items	*Unit*	*95-96*	*96-97*	*97-98*	*Annual Target 98-99 '98*	*Actuals upto Dec/ 98-99*	*Annual estimates for*
1	*2*	*3*	*4*	*5*	*6*	*7*	*8*
EXPORT							
Alumina/ Hydrate	'000MT	415.2	465.13	479.8	425.00	453.68	600
Aluminium	'000MT	49.13	60.36	55.48	60	18.23	30
DOMESTIC							
Aluminium	'000MT	143.09	145.52	140.66	158.00	64.75	120
Power to GRIDCO	MU	1093	903	658	800	718.51	1003

Ongoing projects

Projects under implementation:

Strip Casting Facility

Trial run has started.

Gallium Project :

A 950 Kg/annum 5 N purity Gallium Extraction Plant at Damanjodi at a cost of Rs. 12.77 crore based on indigenous technology and financial assistance to the extent of Rs. 5.54 crore coming from associated Government of India agencies e.g. DSIR, DST, DRDO & NRDC is scheduled to be completed by December, 2000.

Special grade alumina

A 26,400 TPY Special Grade Alumina Plant at Damanjodi, at a cost of Rs. 56.78 crore based on technical know-how obtained from Alumina Technology Associates, USA is expected to be commissioned during the 4th Quarter of 1999.

Zeolite

A 10,000 TPY Detergent Grade Zeolite (Zeolite-A) Plant at Damanjodi at a cost of Rs. 24.10 crore with consultancy services rendered by Engineers India Ltd. is scheduled for completion during the 2nd quarter of 1999.

Aluminium Wheel Project :

The project for setting up of Aluminium Wheel Project for 4,50,000 nos. of wheels per year at Bhubaneswar and 10,000 MT per year Alloy Ingot Plant at Angul is in progress. NALCO has acquired 11.00 acres of land. M/s. MECON has been appointed as an Engineering Consultant. Finalisation of Technology supplier is in advanced stage. The total capital cost is estimated at Rs. 92.56 crores.

Expansion & diversification

Expansion

The proposal for expansion of Aluminium Smelter from 2,30,000 TPY to 3,45,000 TPY and Captive Power Plant from 6 × 120 MW to 7 × 120 MW at a cost of Rs. 2062 crores (June 1997 price level) was approved by the Government of India on 3rd February 1998. M/s Engineers India Ltd. has been appointed as the principal consultant for the expansion of Smelter Project. M/s EIL has also been entrusted with the work of Time & Cost monitoring work.

- M/s M.N. Dastur & Co. has been appointed as the Consultant for implementation of VII unit of CPP.
- An Agreement with M/s Aluminium Pechiney (AP) has been signed on 28.04.98 for supply of basic engineering for certain improvements for the Smelter. This has been approved by SIA in August '98. A team of AP experts visited Angul in June '98 to collect the basic data for preparation of basic engineering. The same has been finalised in August '98.
- The tendering procedure for award of site grading work, provision of power and water for construction are under way and are expected to be awarded shortly.
- The project is to be implemented within 51 months from the zero date viz 3rd Feb '98.

Mines & alumina refinery :

The expansion project for increasing the capacity of Bauxite Mines from 2.4 to 4.8 MTPY and that of Alumina Refinery from 0.8 to 1.575 MTPY at a cost of Rs. 1665 crores is under implementation by the Company. The project is to be implemented within 51 months from zero date i.e. 18th December 1996.

Energy conservation

NALCO has adopted modern technologies in all production units leading to optimal consumption of energy. Best efforts are being made to conserve energy to the maximum extent by constant monitoring of specific energy consumption figures, adopting energy conservation measures, getting energy audit done by in-house team and reputed external professional agencies, encouraging implementation of innovative ideas in this field, exploring possibility of utilisation of renewable energy sources and adopting other useful measures in this direction.

During the year 1997-98, M/sTata Energy Research Institute carried out an energy audit of the Smelter Plant. During the year 1998-99, they are carrying out the energy audit of the Alumina Refinery Plant and Mines.

System support (Railways)

Transportation of bulk raw materials and finished goods are highly dependant on the rail system. All the raw materials like coal, CP coke, caustic soda, furnace oil etc. were transported in sufficient quantities to match the plants requirements. Despatches of alumina for export to Vizag and for Smelter Plant at Angul made upto November '98 are as follows :

By Rail	:	5,67,290 MT
By Road	:	14,165 MT
		5,81,455 MT

The despatches of aluminium metal for the year 1998-99 upto November '98 are as under :

By Rail	:	17,209 MT
By Road	:	60,699 MT
		77,908 MT

As regards coal, a quantity of 1.67 million tonne at Angul and 0.33 million tonne at Damanjodi were handled during this year 1998-99 (upto November '98).

Computerisation

Bauxite mines :

An crder placed on M/s Modular Mining System Inc., USA for Truck Despatch System to monitor and optimise utilisation of loading and hauling equipments. Order execution is in progress.

Alumina refinery : distributor control system

Distributor Control System (DCS) is being implemented along with expansion of Refinery as a part of project activity.

Smelter

Order placed on M/s Digital Equipments (India) Ltd. for implementation of Production Planning and Control System (Metal Planning System). Order execution is in progress.

Captive power plant

Tender evaluation for Plantwide Networking and Supervisory Controlled Data Acquisition System is in progress

Wide area network

To expedite project implementation activities, Wide Area Network Facility extended to M/s Engineers India Ltd. at Gurgaon and M/s Dastur & Co. at Chennai. VSAT installed and operational at EIL, Gurgaon and procurement activity is in progress for VSAT for M/s Dastur & Co.

NSDL

Hardware and software for NSDL operations have been installed. Since July '98, NALCO shares are being traded electronically through NSDL.

Pollution control & environment management efforts

During the year under review, the performance of the Company in pollution control and environmental management has been satisfactory and encouraging. NALCO's efforts have been recognised at national and state levels with Gem Granite Environment Award, 1997-98 and Sitaram Rungta Memorial Social Awareness Award, 1997-98 by FIMI, New Delhi, Pollution Control

Excellence Award, 1998 from Orissa State Pollution Control Board and Best Occupational Health Services Award for M&R complex from State Safety Award Committee, Government of Orissa. Besides NALCO has also received prize money of Rs. 50,000/- for the Indira Priyadarshini Vriskhamitra Award, 1994.

All the 4 units of the Company i.e. Mines, Alumina Refinery, CPP & Smelter have ISO-14001 environment management system certificate. The process has been initiated for implementation of ISO-14001 at Port Facilities, Visakhapatnam.

So far 53,48,150 numbers of trees have been planted at different units of the Company. Out of these 3,91,900 trees were planted during the year 1997-98. The Company has participated in the drinking water supply scheme to 11 villages around the Smelter under peripheral development.

Salient aspect of the work being done by advisory boards/ councils

There are three S&T Advisory Committees in NALCO on the following :

a) Aluminium & Allied Products Project,

b) Alumina & Allied Product Projects and

c) Raw Materials and Allied Products Projects respectively were formed by NALCO, R&D officials academia from prestigious institutions like IIT, BHU, etc., experienced heads of research laboratories and senior level officials from industry to get the best mileage out of interaction and deliberations. The meetings are also structured and planned in a way so that the time of the members are utilised to the maximum.

The committees have no executive powers and are advisory in nature. The committees help in inculcating a process of in house deliberation and problems solving and developing a learning tradition in the organisation. Till date each of the above three committees met three times in a span of two years.

The pooled knowledge of experts and deliberations held in the above committees have helped the Company to go into the nitty gritty of the process parameters alternates available, the practices being followed and optimum solutions. A time table has been drawn for implementation of some of the practical suggestions made by the committees.

Special achievement

Development of this technology has been adjudged as the Best Technology developed during the year 1998 in the chemical discipline and three NALCO's R&D technologists received "NRDC Independence Day Award 1998" for their meritorious invention titled "Process for the Preparation of Alumina Hydrate of Superior Purity and Fineness and Process Preparation of Low Soda High Alpha Pure Alumina". The invention has also been recommended for prestigious WIPO Gold Medal of 1999.

Research & development activities

NALCO's in-house R&D establishments, both at M&R Complex, Damanjodi and S&P Complex, Angul have been recognised by DSIR, Ministry of Science & Technology, Government of India upto 31.3.2000.

Keeping in view, the long term research plans and programmes, medium to short term development activities pertaining to process and product development and adoption of new technologies, revamping of in-house

R&D centres at both Damanjodi and Angul sectors have been successfully completed at a cost of Rs. 5.2 crores.

For the financial year 1997-98, total R&D expenditure as % of turnover comes to 0.367 as compared to 0.029 for the year 1996-97.

Industrial relations

The industrial relations scenario in the Company is characterised by multi-unionism and inter-union rivalry. At present a total sixteen trade unions are functioning at different units out of which five are affiliated to INTUC, four to BMS, two to HMS; the remaining five unions are not affiliated to any Central Trade Union organisation.

There was a breakdown in the Aluminium Smelter of NALCO at Angul, Orissa. NALCO had to shutdown the operation of a number of pots in its smelter plant. Government ordered an Enquiry Committee to look into the problems affecting the smelter of NALCO. The Committee in its conclusion observed poor work culture, improper planning and lack of team work as one of the reasons for the deterioration in the performance of the pots. The Committee made several recommendations to avoid its recurrence. NALCO is taking steps to improve the work culture and discipline in the organisation.

Perspective plan for women's welfare

The Company has on its roll 209 women employees including 39 executives and 170 non-executives. The Company provides equal opportunity to women in employment. However, most of the jobs are highly technical and sufficiently skilled women are often not available for the same.

Necessary amendments have been incorporated I n the Conduct, Discipline Appeal Rules of the Company to combat sexual harassment of women employees. The Company also takes active part in the improvement of quality of social life in the vicinity of its units which includes womenfolk.

Welfare of tribrals and minorities

At Damanjodi, a predominantly tribal area, 521 families who were displaced have been provided with permanent houses in the rehabilitation colony built by the Company with provisions of roads, health and educational facilities, drinking water, electricity and recreation. NALCO has also taken the following welfare measures at its two sites located at Angul and Damanjodi:

i) Direct employment of 439 persons in NALCO on the basis of one able bodied person from each displaced family.

ii) Employment of balance with contractors working in NALCO.

iii) Literacy development programmes for illiterate LDP workers.

iv) In Peripheral Development Plan, an amount of Rs. 259.66 lakhs has been earmarked during the year for development of roads, college, school, library, creation of community centres, adult education centre, renovation of village ponds and wells, development of agricultural land, etc.

A member of the minority community is associated in the Selection Committees for Group "C and D" vacancies as a part of recruitment practice.

Employment of SC/ST/EX-SM/PH/minorities as on 2331/12/ 1998

Group	*Total no. of employees*	*SC*	*ST*	*Ex-SM*	*PH*	*Minorities*
1	*2*	*3*	*4*	*5*	*6*	*7*
Executives	1390	162	71	09	03	62
Non-Executives	4884	900	1055	80	51	169
Trainees	186	33	64	–	01	31
Total	6460	1095	1190	89	55	262

Export/import performance

Details	*Unit*	*95-96 Actuals*	*96-97 Actuals*	*97-98 Actuals*	*Target for 98-99*	*1998-99 Actuals Upto Dec./'98*	*Annual estimate (RE 98-99)*
Calcined Alumina Exports	'000MT	415.2	465.13	479.8	425.00	453.68	600
Aluminium Exports MT	'000MT	49.13	60.36	55.48	60	18.23	30

Mou rating achieved

The Company's performance was rated Excellent in the evaluation of the Memorandum of Understanding signed with Ministry of Steel & Mines, Government of India for last three years. The details of scoring for the last three years is as follows:

Year	*MOU Scoring*	*MOU Rating*
1995-96	1.392	Excellent
1996-97	1.220	Excellent
1997-98	1.452	Excellent

Domestic sales performance

Details	*Unit*	*95-96 Actu-als*	*96-97 Actu-als*	*97-98 Actu-als*	*Target for 98-99*	*1998-99 Actuals Upto Dec./'98*	*Annual estimate (RE 98-99)*
Aluminium	'000MT	143.09	145.52	140.66	158.00	64.75	120.00
Power to GRIDCO	MU	1093	903	658	800	718.54	1003

Progressive use oif Hindi in official work

During the year 1998-99, special efforts were continued towards achieving the targets of progressive use of Hindi in the Company. Original correspondence in Hindi, original work and noting and drafting in Hindi by the employees trained in Hindi was encouraged.

Hindi Week from 8th to 14th September '98 and Hindi Day on 14th September were celebrated with a number of programmes. During this period many Hindi competitions were organised and prizes were distributed to the winners in the closing ceremony observed on 17th September '98.

On the occasion of the Hindi Week, a special issue of the Hindi magazine 'Akshar' was published and prizes were awarded for the best compositions by the employees and officers. Many letters of commendation are received on a national level for the articles published in 'Akshar'.

Publication of Monthly Newsletter Hindi Parichaya is regular. Efforts were made for developing the design and contents of this newsletter and many letters of commendation are being received.

In the Angul sector of NALCO, meetings of the Town Official Language Implementation Committee were organised, which is working under the convenorship of

NALCO and constituted under the directions of Department of Official Language, Ministry of Home Affairs, Government of India. NALCO played a significant role in providing guidance and cooperation in promoting the progressive use of Hindi in the Central Government offices and undertakings of this area.

At Damanjodi sector of the Company, special efforts have been made for increasing the use of Hindi by the employees by organising different Hindi competitions with the assistance of Kendriya Sachivalaya Hindi Parishad.

The challenging task of computerisation originally in bilingual form of different forms used in the office has been taken up by the Hindi Cell of the corporate office. Bilingual designing of most of the forms internally "is continued successfully.

The meeting of Bhubaneswar Town Official Language Implementation Committee was organised on 19th June '98 at Nalconagar auditorium, which was hosted and co-ordinated by NALCO.

Aluminium survey

The financial crises in Asia, Russia and Latin America is expected to undermine growth in the world's developing economies in 1998 as well in 1999. The world GDP growth will be around 1.8% in 1998 down from 3.3% in 1997. The growth is estimated to be 1.7% in 1999.

World aluminium consumption fell by 0.5% in 1998 after achieving a growth of 6.1 % in 1997. The consumption growth is likely to be around 1.3% in 1999.

The Indian primary aluminium production in 1997-98 reached 5,53,000 MT (growth rate of 5.7%) as against 5,23,000 MT (growth rate of 1.5%) in 1996-97. The production in 1997-98 is around 83% of the country's installed capacity of 6,70,000 MT. Projected to grow at a rate of 8%, the aluminium industry in India recorded only around 5.7% in 1997-98 on account of general economic slow down, acute power shortage and low consumption due to financial crisis faced by most of the State Electricity Boards where expansion plans were thereby delayed.

The growth of domestic consumption of aluminium fell sharply to around 2% in 1997-98 from 7% recorded in 1996-97. The growth is expected to be around 4% during the year 1998-99.

Bharat aluminium company limited

Bharat Aluminium Company Limited (BALCO) was incorporated on 27th November, 1965 with an integrated Alumina/Aluminium Complex at Korba in Bilaspur District of Madhya Pradesh. The Aluminium Plant has 200,000 tonnes per annum (TPA) capacity and has been set up based on Soviet Technology. The downstream facilities have the capacity to produce 35,000 TPA of Properzi Rods, 40,000 TPA of Rolled Products, 7,000 TPA of Extrusions and 18,000 TPA of Billets and Slabs etc.

BALCO has a second Unit at Bidhanbag, near Asansol, in West Bengal. This vested in BALCO following nationalisation in June, 1984 by the Government of the company which then owned it.

As on 1st November, 1998 the Authorised Capital of the Company stood at Rs. 500 crores and the Subscribed Capital at Rs. 488.85 crores.

Production performance

The actual production figures of Korba Complex and Bidhanbag Unit for the year 1997-98 along with the target of 1998-99 and actual production figures for April-December, 1998 are given below:

Production performance of Korba/BBU

(Figures in Tonnes)

Item	*1997-98 Actual*	*1998-99 Target*	*April-Dec. '98 Target*	*April-Dec. '98 Actual*
Properzi Rods	30588	42072	31638	26992
Extruded Products	5939	7000	5255	3208
Rolled Products	35786	36000	27135	30036
Ingots, Billets	15885	9000	6722	7456
Total	88198	94000	70750	67692

Bldhanbag unit (BBU)

(Figures in Tonnes)

Item	*1997-98 Actual*	*1998-99 Target*	*April-Dec. '98 Target*	*April-Dec. '98 Actual*
Extruded Products	1004	800	604	284
Rolled Products	954	1500	1131	945
Foils	383	600	451	203
Conductors	84	800	604	–
Others	–	200	149	190
Total	2425	3900	2939	1622

Financial performance

(Rs. in Crores)

Details	*Actual for the previous years estimates 1996-7*	*1997-98*	*Annual budget Dec. 98 Target*	*Actuals upto Actual*
1	2	3	4	5
Income	826.53	859.99	836.77	621.26
Operating Cost	647.23	670.90	646.30	490.67
Interest & Transaction Loss	7.23	6.65	12.30	5.83
Depreciation & amortisation	44.90	47.65	43.15	36.81
Net Profit Before Income Tax & Dividend	127.17	134.79	135.02	94.00

On-going projects and expansion and diversification

New cold rolling mill

The company is implementing a project of setting up a new cold rolling mill at a cost of Rs. 157.50 crores at Korba. On completion of the project, BALCO will have competitive advantage in marketing as this mill would be producing thin sheets and foils.

Mainpet mine

Diversion of 376-924 hectares revenue-forest land for mining (non-forest purpose) had been approved, in principle, by Government of India, Ministry of Environment and Forests. The drilling process in these mines is already on and reserves to the extent of 20 lakh tonnes have been proved. Further results would be known after completion of the remaining drilling process of 18,000 meters.

Rajnandgaon mine

Action for land acquisition has been initiated and M/s. MECON have been appointed to prepare the report for obtaining clearance from Ministry of Environment and Forests for commencement of mining activities.

Captive power plant

Feasibility Report on proposed expansion of the capacity of the Captive Power Plant at Korba is under study in association with NTPC.

(e) The proposal for revamping and modernisation of AAA Conductor Plant, Bidhanbag is under study. Its economic and other related viability aspects have been worked out to facilitate in-depth study in association with Technical Consultants and Experts.

Conservation of energy

Energy Conservation measures taken

Alumina plant

i. improvement of insulation in order to reduce radiation losses.

ii. Descaling of Flash Tank in order to improve the heat economy.

iii. Improvement in the feeding rate of the Hydrate to the Kiln to achieve fuel conservation.

iv. Replacement of Digestor Coils to achieve improvement in heat economy.

Smelter plant

i. Use of compressed air for removal of anode effect in Cell House No. 5 &6. Similarly in Cell House No. 7 & 8.

ii. Reuse of anode paste cooling water by recirculation.

iii. Use of bar breaker for crust breaking.

Fabrication complex

i. Use of fuel oil additive is under trial for conservation of fuel oil in furnaces.

Engineering services

i. In-house efforts for reduction of fuel oil.

ii. The use of E/F grade coal in place of "B" grade coal is under study.

Computerisation

Present Computerisation activity of BALCO includes financial accounting (FA) pay-roll, long-term PF Accounting, long-term PSL Ledger, marketing and invoicing system including excise gatepass, evaluation of ore deposits, etc. Cell House monitoring is also computerised and long-term SCADA is in use.

The Company is also taking necessary steps in its Information Technology Department to develop and make use of information technology in various Departments.

Pollution control & environment protection measures

During the year, the Company planted 10,000 saplings in reclaimed mined out areas. In addition, about 40,000 saplings were also planted in and around Korba and Bidhanbag units.

The Company is making efforts to adopt environment management system to achieve Indian and international standards in environmental management.

Salient aspects of the work being done by advisory board/ Councils

BALCO is presently availing of the technical know how and other related services from Jawaharlal Nehru Aluminium Research Development & Design Centre (JNARDDC), National Environmental Engineering Research Institute (NEERI), Nagpur and Central Glass Ceramic Research Institute (CGCRI), Calcutta.

Research & development

The Company continued its in-house R&D activities in certain specific areas. As a result of such efforts, certain improvements in plant productivity, purity and quality of products have been effected. Besides, development of value added products and cost reductions have resulted from such efforts.

Industrial relations

Industrial relations in the Company remained cordial during the year under review.

Perspective plan for women

Women employees of BALCO are being given all

statutory and normal benefits, including Creche facilities for their children. Seminars and workshops are being organised specially for participation of women employees, apart from sending delegations to outside seminars, etc.

Welfare of tribals & minorities

BALCO is looking after the health and other basic amenities of the surrounding tribal population near the Plant and Mines. Five villages have been adopted by BALCO and basic civic amenities, including health-care, are being given to residents. All other Government directives regarding reservation in employment and other facilities are being followed in the case of tribal population and minorities.

Employment of SC/ST/EX--Sm/PH/LDP/minorities as on 331.12.1998

Group	*Total No. of emplo-yees*	*SC*	*ST*	*Ex Servi-ceman*	*PH*	*LDP*	*Mino-rities*
Executives	1211	78	42	11	7	–	65
Non-Executives	6074	1064	950	92	11	–	674
Management Trainees	–	–	–	–	–	–	–
Apprentice Trainees	181	41	47	–	–	–	1
Total	7466	1183	1039	103	18	–	740

Mou rating

During the last three years the Company has received MOU ratings as follows:-

Year	*MOU Rating*	
1995-96	Very Good	2.27
1996-97	Very Good	2.26
1997-98 (Provisional)	Very Good	1.59

Progressive use of Hindi in official work

The Corporate Office and Korba Complex of the Company are located in "A" Region and its Bidhanbag Unit is in "C" Region. More than 80% of the employees have working knowledge of Hindi. The Corporate and Korba Offices have been, notified under Rule 10(4) of the Official Language Act in all the Units. The percentage of originating correspondence from Corporate Office, Korba Unit to States, individuals and other Central Government Offices in "A" Region is about 85%.

Hindustan zinc limited

Hindustan Zinc Limited (HZL), one of India's leading base metal producers, was incorporated in January, 1966 as a public sector company, after the takeover of the erstwhile Metal Corporation of India Limited~, to develop mining and smelting capacities to substantially meet the domestic demand for zinc and lead metals.

Hindustan Zinc Limited is an MOU signing' Company with Ministry of Steel & Mines, Department of Mines. The performance for 1997-98 was rated as "Excellent".

At present, HZL with its Headquarters at Udaipur operates five lead-zinc mines with a total lead-zinc ore production capacity of 3.04 million tpa and four smelters with combined installed capacity of 152,000 tpa zinc and 65,000 tpa lead, besides a rock phosphate mine. The Company offers a range of zinc and lead metal grades to its customers, besides by-products like silver, cadmium, sulphuric acid etc. The following tables depict the mines and smelters of the Company with corresponding production capacity:

Mines	*ore capacity (TPD)*
Zawar Group of Mines, Distt. Udaipur (Rajasthan)	4000
Rajpura-Dariba Mine, Distt. Rajsamand (Rajasthan)	2400
Rampura-Agucha Mine, Distt. Bhilwara (Rajasthan)	3000*
Sargipali Lead Mine, Distt. Sundergarh (Orissa)	500
Agnigundala Lead Mine, Distt. Guntur (Andhra Pradesh)	240
Maton Rock Phosphate Mine, Distt. Udaipur (Rajasthan)	600

* Mechanical completion of expanded capacity to 4500 tpd.

Smel Ters	*Metal Capacity (TPA)*	
	Zinc	*Lead*
Debari Zinc Smelter, Matt. Udaipur (Rajasthan)	49,000	–
Vizag Zinc & Lead Smelter, Matt. Visakhapatnam (AP)	33,000	22,000
Chanderiya Lead-Zinc Smelter, Distt., Chittorgarh (Raj)	70,000	35,000
Tundoo Lead Smelter, Distt. Dhanbad (Bihar)	–	8,000

Physical performance

Highlights:

1998-99 (April-Dec. 1998):

- Net Profit earning (PBT) of Rs. 107 crore, compared to the budget of Rs. 77 crore.
- Sales turnover of Rs. 897.16 crore, compared to the budget of Rs. 888.25 crore.
- Lead-Zinc concentrate production at 1,03% of the target.
- Zinc metal production at 104% of the target.
- Zinc metal sale at 103% of the target.

The production of lead-zinc ore, concentrate and lead-zinc metals are given below:

(Figures in tonnes)

Product	*1995-96 Actuals*	*1996-97 Actuals*	*1997-98 Actuals*	*Target For 1998-99*	*1998-99 Actuals Upto Dec. '98*	*1998-99 estimate*
1	*2*	*3*	*4*	*5*	*6*	*7*
Lead-Zinc Ore	2398513	2271676	2467729	2620000	2006874	2620000
Lead-Zinc Conc.	350104	336793	353025	402900	312414	390000
ZincMetal	115464	110876	136271	134000	103488	134000
Lead Metal	27843	27874	35766	40500	27856	38500

The lead-zincore and concentrate production are estimated at 100% and 97% respectively of the annual targets.

Zinc and lead metal production are estimated at 100% and 95% respectively of the annual target during the current year.

Financial performance

(Rs. in crores)

Details	*Actual for the previous 3 years*			*Annual Budget Est.*	*1998-99 Actual upto 1998-99 (RE)*	*Annual Estimate 1998-99 Dec.'98 (BE)*
	1995-96	*1996-97*	*1997-98*			
Income	906.83	996.91	1282.13	1197.89	897.16	1233.87
Operating cost	736.21	842.71	996.46	1018.42	733.38	1020.94
Interest	44.05	43.21	26.74	21.06	11.50	15.50
Depreciation	53.51	54.73	57.40	62.41	45.28	61.43
Net Profit (PBT)	65.71	56.22	201.77	96.00	107.00	136.00

During the period ended December, 1998 of the current financial year, the Company had a sales turnover of Rs. 897.16 crore and the profit before tax of Rs. 107 crore compared to the budget of Rs. 888.25 crore and Rs. 77 crore respectively. In view of decline in lead-zinc sale prices, the current financial year is expected to end up with sales turnover of Rs. 1200 crore and net profit of Rs. 136 crore (PBT).

Sales performance

Zinc sales during the period April-Dec. '98 was 96,428 tonnes against a target of 95,500 tonnes. It is expected to end the year with a sale of 129,000 tonnes as per the annual target. The Company expects to export about 45,000 tonnes zinc concentrate during the current year.

Lead sales during the period April-Dec.'98 have been 18,790 tonnes as against a target of 26,000 tonnes. A sale of about 28,000 tonnes is expected during 1998-99 against the annual target of 35,500 tonnes. The shortfall in the sale of lead metal is attributed to higher imports and uncertain market condition, resulting in lower off-take.

New projects

Sindesar Khurd, Distt. Rajsamand, Rajasthan

Sindesar Khurd deposit, near Rajpura Dariba district Rajsamand, Rajasthan has been taken up for development at a cost of Rs. 92 crore as replacement to south lode of R.D. Mine. It will be a satellite mine to Rajpura Dariba Mine and all the infrastructural facilities available including beneficiation plant at RDM will be utilised. An incline is being developed for upgrading the geological results and to confirm lateral continuity of the ore body to obtain geo-technical data and to obtain ore for metallurgical tests on plant scale. The incline has been excavated upto 297.81 mRL, the surface mRL being 510. A level at 350 mRL has been partly developed to provide site for exploratory drilling. Tenders have been invited for sinking of main shaft & excavation of ramp for providing main entry to the mine.

Kayar Lead-Zinc Prospect, Distt. Ajmer

Hindustan Zinc Limited has acquired mining lease of Kayar Lead-Zinc prospect in Ajmer district. A total of 10 million tonnes of geological resource containing 2.67% Pb and 14.89% Zn in three discrete ore bodies has been indicated. In order to establish firm geological, geo-technical and metallurgical parameters and delineate the deposit with fair degree of confidence for preparation of techno-economic feasibility report, an exploration scheme comprising 16800 m of drilling at an estimated cost of Rs. 1 2 crore has been envisaged. Global tenders for executing quality drilling work have been invited and are under evaluation for award of work.

Jagpura gold prospect

As a part of its diversification strategy, HZL is continuing its exploration programme in Jagpura area, District Banswara, Rajasthan, where it holds a prospecting licence (PL) over 43.10 sq. km. Exploratory drilling in progress in the NW an NE blocks has so far outlined an ore resource of 7.99 lac tonnes with 1.91 g/t Gold in oxidized zone and 7.90 lac tonnes with 2.18 g/t Gold in sulphide zone upto a depth of approximately 50 m. The Company has planned to carry out drilling in NE, SW and SE blocks, and to continue mineralogical and metallurgical tests on oxidized/sulphide ore to establish gold recovery process/parameters. An order of magnitude techno-economic study/report is likely to be generated in 1999-2000. In the remaining area of prospecting licence it is planned to carry out ground magnetic survey to identify zones of interest for exploration planning.

Zinc smelter expansion by 10,000 TPA each at Debari and Vizag

Orders were placed for basic engineering for expansion and performance improvement of Debari and Vizag Zinc Smelters on AdZ Technologia, Spain and the draft basic engineering packages have since been submitted. MECON has been appointed for detailed engineering and as consultants for project execution.

Tenders are being issued for execution of the project as per detailed engineering of MECON for carrying out various modifications' and equipment addition for capacity expansion. Award of work and execution of the project is expected to start in the last quarter of 1998-99.

New zinc smelter expansion by 100,000 TPA

The Company's proposal for undertaking a feasibility study at a cost of Rs. 10 crores for setting up of a new Zinc Smelter with a capacity of 60,000 TPA was approved by the Government in September, 1997. The pre-feasibility study commenced in November, 1997.

Based on global tender enquiry, the Company placed an order with M/s. Kvaerner Metal, UK for preparation of the detailed feasibility report for New Zinc Smelter of 100,000 tpa capacity. M/s. EIL has also been appointed to assist the international consultant in preparation of this report. The detailed feasibility report is scheduled to be completed by December 1998/January 1999. Meanwhile the smelter site has been finalised in consultation with senior officials of Rajasthan Government. Preliminary works such as filing of applications for land acquisition under section IV have been taken up.

Nickel extraction technology proving plant

An MOU was signed between HZL and the Council of Scientific & Industrial Research (CSIR) on, the 3rd

September, 1996 for installation of Nickel Technology Proving Plant as a Joint Venture for establishing nickel extraction technology developed indigenously for low grade chromite overburden of Sukinda Valley in Orissa.

Turnkey contracts were awarded for supply and erection of the plant during August, 1998. Foundation stone was laid by the Hon'ble Union Minister of Steel & Mines in September, 1998. The contractor has mobilised at site and civil construction works are under progress. Preparation of detailed engineering drawings and procurement action are under progress, which are expected to be completed by January 1999. Manufacture/ fabrication of equipment at site, shifting of existing equipment and civil structure works are expected to be completed by March, 1999. Erection of equipment is expected to start from mid January, 1999.

International co-operation

HZL -BHPM joint centure

The HZL-BHPM Minerals joint venture for exploration of base and precious metals in Rajasthan has made considerable progress during the year.

Preliminary processing of the airborne geophysical (GEOTEM) survey data was completed and detailed processing and interpretation by BHPM is in progress. The survey has outlined 138 anomalies. Ground checking by geological mapping, geophysics and geochemistry has covered about half of the anomalies. However, on account of the soil covered nature of the terrain, presence of mineralisation can be ascertained only by test drilling.

Based on the results generated, the joint venture has identified areas warranting follow-up.

It is proposed to conduct a second GEOTEM survey over fresh PL application areas, as well as covering parts of existing PLs which could not be flown last year. The survey will involve flying approximately 17,000 line kilometers.

HZL-La source-VIGEGO joint venture

In 1994, the Company entered into a MOU with LaSource (France) and VIGEGO (Vietnam) for a joint venture project to explore and develop the Pac Lang Gold prospect in Vietnam. Approval of the Government of Vietnam, and grant of exploration and prospecting licences (EL/PL) against revised applications, submitted in line with new regulations is awaited. In the meantime, approval of the Government of India was conveyed on 28th December, 1998 to Hindustan Zinc Limited, Udaipur for undertaking the exploration of the Pac Lang Gold prospect in Vietnam in collaboration with LaSource, France. The share of HZIL in the exploration cost shall be 43% of the total cost of exploration. If the exploration work is successful, then feasibility study will be undertaken in collaboration with LaSource. HZL's share in the conduct of feasibility study will be 43%. If the feasibility study leads to setting up of the Joint Venture mining company for exploration of the gold deposit, then the share of the three participating companies will be LaSource-40%, HZL-30% and VIGEGO of Vietnam-30%.

Energy conservation

The Company has been promoting and propagating energy conservation aspects in various facets of its operation. The following measures are being continued in an effort to conserve energy in different plants/mines of the Company.

- Load and Energy management.
- Sizing of equipment.
- Use of energy efficient equipment.

– Accurate measurement and monitoring consumption of various forms of energy.
– Energy audit and survey.
– Optimisation of system power factor Process improvement/modification.

Computerisation

To be in tune with state-of-the-art technology and harness it to business advantage, HZIL has installed a number of Pentium based personal computers with latest software in various functional areas.

It has undertaken the onerous task of solving the year-2000 problem in current application software using in-house expertise and has already carried out the same successfully in a few applications.

8.2 HZL has established connections to the rest of the world electronically by acquiring internet connection at its Head Office and has established e-mail facility'

Pollution control and environment management efforts

Air and water pollution control facilities and plants at all units of the Company are operated regularly to maintain emissions within permissible limits. Regular monitoring of effluents and gaseous emissions has been carried out.

Nearly 8,000 new saplings were planted during the year in addition to the existing trees being kept well maintained at all the mining units of the Company.

Salient aspects of the work being done by advisory boards/ Councils

Joint Consultative Committees are functioning in all major units of the Company. The Committee consists of representatives from workmen and management, and the areas discussed include production and productivity improvement, reduction in cost of production, etc. The recommendations of the Committee are generally implemented.

In addition to the Joint Consultative Committees, various other bipartite committees/fora on Welfare, Safety, Canteen Management, House Allotment, etc. are functioning. The unanimous recommendations of these Committees are also generally implemented. The functioning of these bipartite fora have created a conducive climate for better production/productivity at all levels.

Research and development activities

Development of bioreactor technology

To recover the zinc metal from the Rampura Agucha tails, bioleaching technique has been explored. RRL (Bhubaneswar) was appointed in January, 1998 for developing a process technique for the same. It is proposed to set up a 1 TPD pilot plant at CRDL in which the developed process will be tested.

Manganese nodules

Ocean bed manganese nodules contain about 2% Cu+Co+Ni. Development of process for winning these metals has been in progress at some CSIR Laboratories. At CRDL a process has been developed for generation of nickel-cobalt cake and its dissolution. Further work on pressure leaching has been carried out. Also, a conceptual flowsheet has been worked out for recovering manganese from the leached residue. DOD has selected the process developed by RRL(B) for further scale up in the pilot plant (500 kg/day capacity) to be set up at CRDL.

Recovery of germanium

Various residues generated from HZL's smelters are being identified to find out potential germanium sources. Samples have been collected from the smelters for estimation of germanium. Analysis carried out by C-

MET, Hyderabad are quite encouraging. A joint venture between HZL and C-MET is being planned in this regard.

Industrial relations

The industrial relations in the Company during the period remained cordial and peaceful.

Women's welfare

The female employees of the Company are given better welfare amenities. They are also being sent for training, both in-house and outside. Participation by female employees in various national fora is also being organised.

The Company has female doctors in the hospitals/ dispensaries.

Welfare of tribals and minorities

Various welfare measures including free medical aid, drinking water, school facilities, co-operative/provision store facilities, etc. are being made available/extended to the tribals and minorities residing in the adjacent areas of the unit.

Employjment in the company

(As on 31.12.1998)

Group	*Total No. of Employees*	*SC*	*ST*	*EX-SM*	*PH*
Executives	1510	103	23	6	3
Non-Executives	10308	1718	1497	218	69
Management Trainees	69	8	2	–	–

Export/import performance

Export

The Company expects to export about 45000 tonnes zinc

concentrate during the current year. Import:

(Rs. in Lakh)

Import	*1997-98 (Estimated)*	*1998-99*
Raw material	17784.36	3723.00 (Approx.)
Components, stores & spares	3720.63	1433.00
Capital goods	321.88	300
Total	5826.87	5456.06

Mou ratings

The MOU ratings achieved by the Company during the last three years are given below:

1995-96 – Very good

1996-97 – Very good

1997-98 – Excellent

Use of Hindi

Progressive use of Hindi (April-Nov., 1998)

100% compliance of Section 3(3) of the Official Language Act has been followed in all the units including the Head Office.

The situation of Hindi correspondence of the various units is as follows:

HO-32%, CRDL-39%, Debari-45.3%, Maton Mine - 65.8%, Zawar Mines-77.5%, Dariba Mine-71.8%, Chanderiya 30.5%, Agucha Mine-29.9% and Tundoo Smelter-29.6%.

Non-Hindi speaking units: Vizag - 62.1%, Agnigundala Mine - 31% and Sargipali Mine - 44.3%.

Four employees appeared in Hindi typing examination conducted under Hindi Teaching Scheme of the Government.

Twenty Hindi workshops were organized from time to time in all the units of the Company in which 173 employees participated.

Hindi day/week has been celebrated effectively in all the units. On this occasion Rajbhasha seminars/ competitions/Hindi workshops were organized.

Active cooperation is extended to Udaipur Town Official Language Implementation Committee, constituted by Rajbhasha Vibhag (Govt. of India).

The branches of Kendriya Sachivalaya Hindi Parishad, Now Delhi are active in several units including Head Office and various competitions have been organized from time to time.

Official Language Implementation Committees have been formed in all the units of the Company and quarterly meetings are held regularly.

Following number of employees were awarded under the various incentive schemes:

(i)	Hindi Teaching Scheme (Hindi teaching)	25
(ii)	Hindi Teaching Scheme (Hindi Typing/Stenography)	6
(iii)	Hindi Cheque Incentive Scheme	6
(iv)	Monthly Allowance Scheme for Hindi typing/stenography	49
(v)	Financial Incentive Scheme for use of Hindi	4

Hindustan Copper Limited

Hindustan Copper Limited (HCL) was incorporated on 9th November, 1967, under the Companies Act, 1956. It was established as a Government of India enterprise to take over, from National Mineral Development Corporation Ltd., all plants, projects, schemes and studies pertaining to the exploration and exploitation of copper deposits, including smelting and refining, for fulfilling long-term objectives of the nation, viz. development and growth of copper mining industry on sound lines and to maximise indigenous production of copper metal. This is to be achieved by developing new copper deposits, known or to be discovered, by adopting appropriate and modern technologies.

The Government of India nationalised the only copper producing company, Indian Copper Corporation Ltd. at Ghatsila in Bihar in March 1972 and handed over i management and ownership to HCL.

In November 1982, the prestigious Malanjkhand Copp Project comprising of a large and fully mechanise open pit mine and Concentrator plant was dedicated t the nation.

The Continuous Cast Copper Rod plant at Taloja Copper Project of Hindustan Copper Ltd. was commissioned in December, 1989 with an installed capacity of 60,000 T. The Company has selected Southwire SCR-2000 technology using natural gas as fuel.

Mines

Location of Mines	*Ore Capacity (TPD)*
Khetri Copper Complex, Rajasthan	19.50 lakh tonnes per annum
Indian Copper Complex, Bihar	11.02 lakh tonnes per annum
Malanjkhand Copper Project, Madhya Pradesh	20.00 lakh tonnes per annum

Smelters

Location of mines	*Metal capacity (TPA)*
Khetri Copper Complex, Rajasthan	31000 tonnes per annum
Indian Copper Complex, Bihar	16500 tonnes per annum

Physical performance

.1 The production of ore, metal in concentrates, refined copper (cathode) and wire rod during the year 1997-98 and 1998-99 are given below:

Details	*Actual for the previous 3 years*			*Annual Budget Est. 1998-99 (BE)*	*1998-99 Actual upto Dec.'98*	*Annual Estimate 1998-99 (RE)*
	1995-96	*1996-97*	*1997-98*			
1	*2*	*3*	*4*	*5*	*6*	*7*
Ore Production ('000 tonnes)	4690	3893	4496	4090	3192	4090
Metal in Concentrates (T)	46563	37271	41440	37080	28875	37080
Refined Copper (Cathode) (T)	41153	38481	42374	43500	28703	35500
Wire rod (Taloja) (T)	37280	41332	31484	36600	25989	30800

Financial performance (operating results)

Details	*Actual for the previous 3 years*			*Target for 1998-99*	*1998-99 Actual upto Dec.'98*	*1998-99 Estimated*
	1995-96	*1996-97*	*1997-98*			
1	*2*	*3*	*4*	*5*	*6*	*7*
Income	1133.68	1001.05	807.05	890.27	545.47	741.90
Operating Cost	963.03	1037.16	849.70	870.05	625.09	790.06
Interest and Transaction loss	39.66	40.67	58.89	49.17	49.12	66.67
Depreciation and Amortisation	55.15	53.84	68.46	62.90	33.14	57.35
Net Profit before income tax & dividend	75.84	(130.62)	(169.72)	(91.85)	(161.68)	(172.18)

Capital restructuring

The Company has been incurring huge losses for the last two years mainly due to drastic fall in LME price of copper and reduction of customs duty on import of copper. To revive this important PSU, the Department has initiated a number of measures which include, inter alia, restructuring the capital base of the Company. The government has accorded approval to the proposal of capital restructuring of HCL seeking:

(i) The outstanding Government loan of Rs. 180.73 crores with M/s HCL as on 31.3.98 may be converted into 7.5% non-cumulative redeemable preference shares to be redeemed at the end of 10th year from the date of conversion and waiver of the outstanding interest as on 31.3.1998 amounting to Rs. 167.43 crores.

(ii) Raising of working capital term loans from Financial institutions/Banks by HCL to the tune of Rs. 75 crores against Government of India (GOI) guarantee for meeting its cash losses for the current financial year i.e. 1998-99.

(iii) A non-plan loan qf Rs. 414 crores be given to HCL for VRS at 14.5% rate of interest with a moratorium of 3 years on repayment of principal and interest and repayment of principal amount in subsequent twelve years for separation of 11043 employees of HCL during the years 1998-99 to 2001-2002. If, even after 2 years, the LME price of copper is less than $1850 per MT, Ministry of Finance (Department of Expenditure) will review the period of moratorium extended to HCL. The moratorium period will not be reviewed if

HCIL faces a repayment problem due to its own inefficiency.

Action has been initiated to implement the above decision.

Sales performance

The Company achieved a total sale of 57,857 tonnes during the year 1997-98. The Company is likely to achieve a total sale of around 50,460 tonnes of copper during 1998-99.

Expansion

Expansion of Khetri Smelter and Refinery

HCL's proposal for expansion of Khetri Smelter and Refinery from 31,000 tpa to 1,00,000 tpa, which was awaiting government clearance, has been dropped owing to the financial performance of the Company. HCL has taken up technological upgradation/debottlenecking scheme of KCC Smelter and Refinery leading to enhancement of the capacity from 31000 tpa to 45000 tpa which would fit into the overall objective of raising the capacity ultimately to 1,00,000 tpa. The Government has given clearance to go ahead with the above scheme. For implementation of the above scheme, discussions have been initiated with Outokumpu Engineering Contractors Oy (OEC), Finland. Similar action has been planned for increasing the capacity of ICC Smelter from the present 16,500 to 25,000 tpa.

Energy conservation

Copper extraction is an energy intensive operation. Special attention is given in making the operation energy efficient at all stages starting from mining of ore to extraction of metal. Due to energy conservation awareness and regular monitoring on consumption of all energy inputs, HCL has been able to maintain the norms of consumption.

Constant thrust is also maintained on improvement of power factor. Improvement in power factor during last three years is tabulated below:

Units	*1996-97*	*1997-98 (Upto Dec'98)*	*1998-99*
KCC	0.92	0.93	0.94
ICC	0.89	0.90	0.915
MCP	0.97	0.98	0.993

. Computerisation

There has been further progress in computerisation in HCL during the current year 1998-99. Most of the system development work started in the year 1997-98, has been completed.

The computer resources have also been augmented in the units and offices mainly to replace the old PCs with the advanced type to take care of the increasing load of work and new jobs.

Internet uses have been initiated between Head Office and other regional offices and projects.

The computerisation effort has been strengthened by further decentralizing. Some integrated system design and development is being carried out by Systems Department with the idea of standardization among the offices.

The software packages, that had been made internally for financial, stores and commercial jobs, are being made ready for the year 2000 compliance.

Pollution control and environment management efforts

Air and water pollution control facilities and plants at all units of the Company operated regularly to maintain emissions within permissible limits. Regular monitoring of effluents and gaseous emissions has been carried out.

Salient aspects of the work being done by advisory boards/ councils

Well established system of employees participation in management in the units as well as at the corporate level are functioning. Shop Councils in each shop and joint councils at unit levels besides bipartite committees on Safety, Canteen, Grievance Handling, House allotment and Housekeeping are in existence and functioning properly. These Committees are attended by Senior Executives and union leaders and they discuss issues on production, productivity, welfare, training and other allied matters of industrial value. Meetings are held at regular intervals - every month and every three months at other committee quite often as the case may be.

At the corporate level, there are two apex committees. These are National Joint Committee for Copper (NJCC) which deals with welfare, medical and social facilities wages and service conditions etc. of workers for the Company as a whole on a national level and meet at regular intervals. The other is Joint Consultative Committee (JCC) which meets once in a quarter to discuss the issues on production and productivity, cost control, yields, safety, pollution control measures etc. These are attended by Chairman-cum-Managing Director, Directors and all the Unit Heads, Personnel Heads from the management side and very senior leaders from the workmen side.

Research and development activities

The Government of India stopped financing R&D activities of HCL from the year 1997-98 in accordance with the decision taken under financial guidelines for R&D activities of PSUs. HCL was also under acute financial crisis during the year under review. However, the Company maintained its thrust in science and technological activities also during the year 1997-98. This resulted in the following two major achievements:

Nickel electro winning

Successful development of Process Flow Sheet for extraction of associated Nickel from Copper ore and production of commercial grade electro-won Nickel cathode. A pilot plant of capacity to produce 1 tonne of Nickle cathode per month based on this process route was set up at ICC during the year. During the year under review, 3 tonnes of Nickel cathodes was produced at ICC. The plant is currently being scaled up to a production capacity of 5 tonnes per month of Nickel cathode.

Hydrometallurgical route of copper extraction

Leachability of Chalcopyrite concentrate with recovery of copper to more than 95% along with extraction of gold, silver, sulphur etc. as by - products, has been established through in-house R&D activities and also through test work carried out by Mintek, South Africa. Establishment of Flow Sheet with detailed design and development of pilot scale operating plant is currently being pursued-

Industrial relations

The industrial relations situation indifferent units of Hindustan Copper Limited was by and large peaceful. The Government order to close down the Mosaboni Mines including Badia, under Industrial Disputes Act, 1947 was challenged by the different unions operating at Mosaboni Mines in the Hon'ble High Court, Calcutta as well as at Hon'ble High Court, Patna, Ranchi Bench. After prolonged legal battle in the High Court, the judgement of the Calcutta High Court went in favour of the management. The union filed Special Writ Petition in the Hon'ble Supreme Court against the judgement of the Division Bench of Calcutta High Court which was dismissed by the Apex Court. Hon'ble High Court of Patna, Ranchi Bench had earlier modified its judgement by vacating the stay on the closure of the mines.

After dismantling and salvaging of equipment, Mosaboni Mines has been closed with effect from 28th September, 1998. Though separate groups belonging to different unions and political parties resorted to agitation for rehabilitation and redeployment of the remaining workmen of the Mosaboni Mines, now closed. The Nominee Action Committee resorted to agitation demanding and voicing their grievances for induction of the nominees of the employees who had died in harness. The casual workmen whose services were dispensed with also were involved in dharna and agitation demanding their engagement.

Mrs. Abha Mahato, Hon'ble local MP, who paid a visit to Calcutta and had detailed discussion with the management, was apprised of the problems being faced by the Company.

Perspective plan for women's welfare

Implementation of equal remuneration act

In Hindustan Copper Limited, no discrimination is made with regard to sex, caste, creed between male and female employees. Persons doing similar nature of job get equal remuneration.

Equality of opportunity in employment and recognition of the right to work as a fundamental right guaranteed by the constitution.

As per Mines Act, 1952, employment of women in underground is prohibited. In other areas, employment to women is provided. In Hindustan Copper Limited equal opportunity is provided and no discrimination is made between male and female employees. In promotion no discrimination is made and women are considered at par, subject to recruitment and promotion rules of the Company.

Application of maternity benefit act to women

Provision of Maternity Benefit Act are strictly followed in Hindustan Copper Limited.

Training facilities at the place of work on new machinery

Wherever new machineries like electronic typewriters are introduced, women employees are provided with necessary training to equip them to operate the machines.

In - company training programme

Women employees attend various in-company training programmes like adult education, workers development seminars and general development programmes organised periodically at unit training centres. Women employees were also given in service training.

Creche facilities

Creche facilities are provided to the women at the project.

Welfare of tribals and minorities

The main welfare activities in respect of Tribal and Minorities are the part of 20 point Programme of the Company. The following activities were undertaken during the period April to October, 1998:

Clean drinking water

Repair of existing tubewells at different projects and construction of 'Bandh' at KCC. 950 persons were benefitted.

Health for all

Regular multi diagnostic camp at surrounding villages. 183 children were immunised and 450 persons were medically checked up.

Expansion of education

More than 8 adult education centres run by the Company through Mahila Samaj. Relevant stationery and books are distributed to the participants free of cost. 125 persons were benefited.

Employment of SC/ST/EX-servicemen/PH/LDP/minorities as on 31-12-98

Group	*Total no. of employees*	*SC*	*ST*	*Ex-service men*	*PH*	*LDP*	*Minorities*
Executives servicemen	1904	170	51	22	6	–	101
Non-Executives	16236	2367	2866	729	126	1288	1077
Trainees:							
(i) Trade Apprentices		268					
(ii) GET	–	Nil					
(iii) MT	–	1					

Mou rating of PSUs achieved

1995-96 – Very Good
1996-97 – Fair
1997-98 – Fair

Progressive use of Hindi in official work

During the period April to October, 1998, concerted efforts were made to achieve the targets fixed by the Government of India regarding progressive use of Hindi. Special emphasis was laid on employees to use their working knowledge of Hindi in day to day official work.

Check points were made more effective to ensure 100% compliance of Section 3(3) of Official Language Act.

Special Incentive Scheme for Noting and Drafting originally in Hindi continued during the period. Hindi workshops were organised and Hindi Fortnights/Weeks were celebrated in all the units including Head Office. During the year the third sub-committee of Parliamentary Committee on Official Language inspected our Head Office. The Committee expressed its satisfaction at the work being done to promote the Official Language in HCL. The 50th Anniversary of India's Independence was celebrated in all our projects and Head Office with great enthusiasm. On this occasion, various programmes/competitions were held wherein our employees and their family members participated in large numbers. A crossword puzzle scheme has been introduced by Head Office during the period to create interest in Hindi among the employees. This has been welcomed by all the employees. During the period April to October, 1998 our Head Office was awarded with a letter of appreciation for best compliance in regard to official language policy of the Government of India by CALTOLIC.

The Official Language Implementation Committee chaired by the CMD at Head Office and the Executive Directors at units, held their meetings regularly in which constraints in implementation of Official language were discussed and measures for their removal were worked out. A new switch latest P.C. word processor was installed for Hindi Department at the Head Office for development of Official Language.

Four Manuals of the Company viz. Stores Manual, Trainer's Manual, Standing Rules for RCP and ICC have been printed on new P.C.

On the occasion of Hindi Day, the message of CMD was distributed in all the offices and units on 14th September, 1998.

Annual Hindi Programme was organised wherein prizes were distributed to the winners of various competitions held on the progressive use of Hindi. Hindi classes were conducted and employees took the Hindi statutory examination held by the Ministry of Home Affairs.

Bharat gold mines limited

Bharat Gold Mines Limited (BGML) became a Public Sector Undertaking under the Department of Mines in 1972. It is primarily engaged in mining in its captive mines in Kolar Gold Fields (KGF), Karnataka and Andhra Pradesh and production of gold in KGF. As a diversification measure, the Company also undertakes mine construction, shaft sinking, manufacture of mining machinery and other fabricated items for outside clients for which it has set up a Mine Construction and Engineering Division.

Present scenario

BGML is a sick company and is before the Board for Industrial and Financial Reconstruction (BIFR) since 1992. During June, 1997 the Government decided, inter-alia, to explore the possibility of rehabilitating BGML through joint venture route by induction of a private co-promoter(s). Accordingly, a Committee was constituted, which has since given its report. The future of BGML will be decided as per the provisions of Sick Industrial Companies (Special Provisions) Act, 1985.

Financial performance

The authorised share capital of the Company is Rs. 60 crores and paid up share capital is Rs. 51.06 crores as on 31.3.1998. The working results of the Company for the last two years and current year upto December, 1998 are as follows:-

		Loss (Rs. in lakhs)
1996-97	:	5379.94
1997-98	:	3983.40
1998-99 (upto Dec., 1998)	:	4992.74

Production performance

The quantity of ore milled, gold and silver extracted during 1997-98 and 1998-99 (April - Dec., 1998) are given below:

	Actual 97-98	*Target for 98-99 (Revised)*	*April-Dec., 98 (Actual)*	*Jan. 99 to Mar., 99 (Anticipated)*
Ore Miled (Tonnes)	151.381	174.470	115.085	59.385
Gold Extracted (Kg.)	514.17	550.00	404.1	145.90
Extraction Grade (g/t)	3.24	3.03	3.36	–
Silver Exttracted (kg.) (by-product)	43.90	–	32.10	–

Sources of funding

As the Company is continuously incurring losses and unable to generate any internal resource, the investment on the capital schemes is met by the Government as Plan loans. The Government has approved an outlay of Rs. 450.00 lakhs as Plan loan towards the capital expenditure during 1998-99. Besides, the Government has provided for non-plan loan of Rs. 16.55 crores during the current year.

Diversification

The Company is diversifying its activities in the following fields:

i) Shaft Sinking and Mine Construction.

ii) Manufacture of mining equipment and fabrication and machining of components.

Shaft sinking and mine construction

The Projects and Contracts Division established in 1973 has been taking contract jobs in shaft sinking and mine construction activities for various mining companies in both coal and metallic ore mines in the country.

The Division has so far completed 68 jobs valued at Rs. 107.74 crores for its customer companies spread all over the country. It is executing 5 contracts at present valued at Rs. 23.30 crores. In addition, contracts valued at Rs.13.00 crores are under negotiations.

This Division endeavours to maximise its revenue thereby sharing the Company's fixed costs. The company envisages undertaking contracts of high value and to execute the jobs by sub-contracting to local contractors wherever possible to cut down operating costs.

Manufacture of mining equipment and fabrication of components

As part of the diversification activity and to generate additional revenue from the workshops, engineering jobs are undertaken viz. manufacture and sale of mining machinery and equipment like winders, suspension gears, head gear, man-riding systems, skips, ore-bins, various safety gadgets, battery operated locomotives, mine car circuit systems, material handling systems, electro winning cells, "GOLD DRILL", TCT rods, etc., besides jobbing work like fabrication and machining for other major industries.

The Engineering Division has achieved a production value of Rs.220.71 lakhs during April, 98 to Dec., 98 besides catering to its captive needs of the metallurgical and mining operations at KGF and other project sites all over India. The production value for the year 1998-99 is estimated at Rs.400.00 lakhs.

The Engineering Division has secured orders worth Rs.313.64 lakhs during April 98-Nov 98. BGML has been awarded, as a result of their participation in a tender process, developmental order for 60 nos Boxn Type Wagons in February 1998 for a total value of Rs.297.79 lakhs of which three proto-type wagons have to be manufactured and approved by the RDSO, Bangalore, before executing the balance quantity. Necessary infrastructure facilities have been completed and orders for certain critical bought-out items like bogie, couplers, draftgear, braking system etc. have been placed. After approval of 3 proto-type wagons by RDSO, the balance 57 wagons would be taken up in the second phase to complete the work order in full.

Achievement during 1998-99

The sales made upto October 1998 and orders position on hand by end of Dec., 1998 are as follows-

(Rs. in lakhs)

Description No.	*Orders on hand value*	*Cumulative orders executed (April-Dec. 1998)*
T.C.T. Drill Rods	18.32	26.15
Workshop Sales	1018.83	194.56
Total	1037.15	220.71

Exploration activies

Chigargunta mine, Chittoor District, AP

The primary level development activities were continued in 4th level of IIIE & IVE Block and 5th level of South Boundary Block on E-2 lode. The ore body delineation works were continued in VE Block. In addition to the above, the stope preparatory development works were carried out in different blocks on E-2 lode.

Old bisanatham mine, Chittoor District, AP

The primary level development works were carried out in 260', 350' and 425' levels north of Downnight shaft. Stope preparatory developments i.e. finger raises and sub-level were carried out between 260' and 425' levels.

Nundydroog mine, Kolar gold fields, Karnataka

The underground developments were related to mainly slope preparatory works in the form of sub-levels and raises in G (Top), G (bottom) and J (North) sections.

Yeppamana mine, Anantapur District, AP

There was no primary level development. The underground development related to stope preparatory works in the form of sub-level, raises and orebody stripping to convert the stope block ready for production between 6th and 7th levels in BG ore shoot of the mine.

Geological services

Geological services were extended to sampling in mills, metal balance studies and updating the status of ore reserves of the mines.

Environmental protection

The Company has taken up afforestation programme on tailing dumps as a pollution control measure and on the barren lands to improve the ecology in a phased manner. Different species like Eucalyptus, Sandalwood, Accacia, Aurculiformis Sissoo, Bevu, Honge, etc., have been planted over 3230 acres of land so far at Kolar Gold Fields and Gadag in Karnataka and Ramgiri, Old Bisanatham and Chigargunta in Andhra Pradesh.

Pollution control

Domestic water treatment

The effluent after treatment is collected in the oxidation ponds constructed in Mysore Mine, Champion Reef and Nundydroog mine areas. These works have been carried out as per the recommendations of Karnataka State Pollution Control Board and National Environmental Engineering Research Institute. A Water Treatment plant has been setup at Chigargunta mine to provide potable water to the employees.

Industrial effluent treatment

Additional three bunds to prevent overflow of slurry, have been constructed over the tailing bund at Nundydroog Mill area. One earthen dam has been constructed near Mysore Mine dump area to prevent washing away of tailings due to rain.

Industrial relations

Welfare of SC/ST tribals and minorities

There are directives/guidance from the Ministry of Social Justice and Empowerment with regard to preparation of sub-component plan for Scheduled Caste and tribal sub-plan for Scheduled Tribes. This is linked with rehabilitation of tribals on account of land acquired for the project. BGML has not acquired any land causing displacement of tribals for the construction of projects and hence no plan for rehabilitation has been drawn.

Minority group members have been nominated to represent in recruitment and promotion committees to safeguard the interest of minority groups. Their grievances are promptly attended to and settled.

Recruitment of minorities and SC/STs in the PSEs

During the period, no recruitments were made.

Employment of SC/ST as on 31.12.1998

Group	Total employee	SC	%	ST	%
A	123	27	21.95	4	3.25
B	30	8	26.66	–	–
C	2342	920	39.28	18	0.77
D	1871	1100	58.79	23	1.26
Total	4366	2055	47.06	45	1.03

No. of employees

Technical & Non Technical as on 31.12.1998 were as follows:

Technical	—	2311
Non-Technical	—	2006
Total	—	4317

Family welfare measures

Perspective plan for women's welfare

As a part of 20 point programme, a separate cell known as Community Development Cell was formed in 1987 to encourage certain self-employment programmes. At present 40 ladies are engaged in weaving, manufacture of handgloves, helmet, liners, phenyl, etc.

Power consumption

There was an increasing trend in the consumption of power during the period April to October 1998 by 6.14% as compared to the previous year. The details of power consumption are given below:

Progress made in the use of Hindi in the enterprise

The Company has made satisfactory progress in the propagation of Hindi as per the provisions of Official

Language Act and Rules made thereunder during the year 1998-99. Incentive schemes of the Government of India have been implemented. The employees who have typed their Official Letters in Hindi were awarded special incentives under Quarterly Hindi Typewriting Incentive Scheme. To popularise Hindi among employees, competitions in Hindi Shorthand, Noting and Drafting, Letter writing and Essay were conducted. The Hindi Diwas was celebrated on 14th September, 1998.

Year	*Units consumed (in lakhs)*	*Anticipated increase during 1998-99*	*% of anticipated increase during the year (lakhs units)*
1997-98 (April-March)	353.24	42.45**	12%
1998-99 (April-March)		*395.69	

* Actual consumption from April to October 1998 and estimate for November 1998 to March 1999.

** The increase in consumption of power was mainly due to pumping operation from mines at KGF.

Sadhbhavana day pledge

All employees of BGML collectively took the pledge at their respective working places on 31.8.1998 (Sadhbhavana Diwas) to work with dedication and desist from violence and resolved to solve all their grievances by peaceful and Constitutional means.

Sikkim mining corporation

The Sikkim Mining Corporation was established by a proclamation of the then Darbar of Sikkim in February, 1960 as a joint venture having 51% equity from Government of Sikkim and 49% equity from Government of India. After a gestation period of about 6 years, production of the complex ore from Bhotang Mine started since 1966-67 onwards. This was the only mine till recently in the country which produced three metals (copper, lead and zinc) from a polymetallic complex ore. There is also the presence of appreciable amount of silver and some amount of gold in the ore. As on 1.4.98 the mine is estimated to have (proved & probable) reserves of about 3.28 lakh tonnes and has already produced about 4.11 lakh tonnes of ore since its inception. Currently Bhotang mine is producing about 54 TPD (tonnes per day) of ore and the other exploratory mine called 'Pacheykhani', located about 15 km away from the former in the East Sikkim district, is also producing about 18 TPD. The cumulative production would be enhanced to 90-100 TPD after the major repair of the existing Cone Crusher of the Mill plant by the end of the financial year 1998-99. The copper concentrate produced by the corporation is sold of to M/s Hindustan Copper Ltd., zinc concentrate to M/s Hindustan Zinc Limited and lead consentrate is not saleable at present due to high bismuth (0.6 to 0.7%) content which contains appreciable amount of silver. The performance of the Corporation has never been good due to various reasons but recent capital re-structuring proposal already approved by the Board of Directors for enhancing the Share Capital from Rs.6.00 crores to Rs.10.00 crores is expected to result in improvement of its productivity and financial performance in near future.

Mines

Location of Mines	*Ore Capacity (TPD)*
1. Bhotang Multimetal Mine	100 TPD (Currently 54 TPD)
2. Pacheykhani Copper Mine (Both located in East Sikkim)	20 TPD (Currently 18 TPD)

Physical performance

The production of Sikkim Mining Corporation during the year 1997-98 and 1998-99 are given below :

(in Tonnes)

Product	*1995-96*	*1996-97*	*1997-98*	*1998-99 Target*	*1998-99 Actuals (Prov.)*
Ore	11026	9685	15698	20020	18000
Concentrate					
1. Copper	206	321	791	1020	1020
2. Lead	499	372	90	100	100
3. Zinc	359	337	289	20	12

On-going projects

The projects which are in progress at Bhotang Mine include :-

i) Deepening of present shaft from 3rd level to 4th level and ultimately upto 5th level under capital development along with shaft winder equipment like extension and conversion of the Air Winder to Electrical system (Approx. cost Rs. 7.00 lakhs)

ii) Owing to high cost of reliable and imported Cone Crusher, the idea of procuring a new one has been dropped and the old Cone Crusher has been given for capital repair at a cost of Rs. 11.24 lakhs and is likely to be in operation by the end of the financial year 1998-99.

iii) Capital mine development in deeper level (below 5th level) and extension in strike direction towards South, below river Tista for increasing ore reserve base is in progress. A parallel drive has also been started at 3rd level to enable exploitation of the ore available at the same level for mineral conservation.

Financial performance

Operating results

Details	*Actuals for the previous years 95-96*	*96-97*	*97-98*	*Annual Budget Estimate 1998-99*	*Actual (Prov.)*
Income	56.81	89.68	105.30	155.00	160.00
Operating Cost	81.70	97.83	107.29	141.00	137.00
Interest & Transaction Loss	15.76	50.52	14.00	–	9.00
Depreciation & Amortisation	13.97	13.37	13.00	14.00	14.00
Net Profit Before Income Tax & Dividend	(–)54.62	(–)72.04	(–)28.29 (Prov.)	–	–

Expansion and divesification

Expansion

In order to make the Corporation flexible and more viable another exploratory mine called "Pacheykhani" (located at about 15 km away in same East Sikkim district) has been started w.e.f. 2nd May, 1997 onwards and is producing about 18 TPD of monometal (copper) ore which is being procesed at Bhotang Mine plant. This mine is still under capital development and the production capacity is to be enhanced to about 30 TPD.

New scheme (diversification)

The organisation has applied for one Coal lease at Kamling in West Sikkim district as a part of the diversification programme. In addition to it, the organisation is likely to apply for another copper deposit (already proved) at Dikchu/upper Pacheykhani and other valuable minerals of the State.

For better conservation of minerals and enabling higher grades of concentrates as an end product, the management has planned to set up one Vertical Columner floatation process after enhancement of Share Capital.

In order to ensure safe underground working below river Tista as well as to enhance qualitative production of R.O.M. from Bhotang Mine, a stowing plant would be installed at a capital cost around Rs. 10.00 lakhs during the financial year for which necessary action has already been initiated. The system will also contribute towards environment preservation due to processing of Mill Tailing and sending it back to the underground mine for back filling at cut and fill method of stopping.

Energy conservation

The Corporation has installed one low tension (440 V) on line Voltage Stabilizer/Controller on 16th June, 1998 on capital expenditure of more than Rs. 8.00 lakhs to maintain industrial voltage level of 400+1% against fluctuating supply voltage of 300 to 460 volts. It is functioning successfully and is not only safe-guarding the electrical equipment but has also improved the power factor appreciably.

Industrial relations

Cordial, peaceful and harmonious industrial relationship prevail between the management and the workers of the Corporation.

Prospective plant for women welfare

For the welfare of women, the Corporation is running a Carpet Weaving Centre under the guidance and supervision of SMC Employees' Co-operative Society Ltd. from where many women/girls were imparted training mostly amongst the wives and dependents of the SMC employees with a view to make them self-sufficient. A number of women have taken advantage of this scheme and now some of them are doing the job independently.

Welfare of tribal and minorities

Every possible efforts has been made by the Corporation for the welfare of the tribal and minorities working in the Corporation.

Employment of SC/ST/EX-SM/PH/LPD/minorities as on 31.12.1998

Group	*Total*	*SC No. of employee*	*ST*	*EX-SM*	*PH*	*LDP*	*Minori--ties*
Executive	6	–	2	–	–	–	–
Non-Executive	234	22	62	3	–	–	–
Trainees	–	–	–	–	–	–	–
Total	240	22	64	3	–	–	–

11

Science and Technology Programme

The Science and Technology Programme of the Department was initiated in 1978. The activities under the Science & Technology Programme in the mineral and non-ferrous metal sectors cover the fields of geology, exploration, mining and environment, bioleaching, beneficiation, rock mechanics, ground control and non-ferrous metallurgy.

The projects are based on (a) national requirement, (b) industry requirement, and (c) requirement of Public Sector Undertakings. The projects are approved by the Standing Scientific Advisory Group (SSAG) of the Department under t e Chairmanship of Secretary (Mines). The Department of Mines provides support to different organisations as well as the Public Sector Undertakings for implementing the S&T Programme.

Financial outlay

The outlay for the S&T Programme was Rs.8.50 crores (Budget Support Rs. 4.00 crores) for 1998-99. This has been revised to Rs. 7.16 crores (Budget Support Rs.3.00 crores) in the R.E. for 1998-99. The Budget Support of Rs.3.00 would be utilised. An outlay of Rs.9.45 crores (Budget Support Rs. 4.00 crores) has been proposed for 1999-2000.

Centres of excellence

Three Centres of Excellence were set up under the S&T Programme of the Department in the areas of (i) Bauxite, Aluminium and Alumina technology, (ii) Rock Mechanics and Ground control and (iii) Occupational health hazards faced by miners due to their long exposure to the mining environment. The Centres are:-

I. Jawaharlal Nehru Aluminium Research Development and Design Centre, Nagpur,

II. National Institute of Rock Mechanics, Kolar Gold Field, and

III. National Institute of Miners' Health, Kolar Gold Field.

Jawaharlal Nehru aluminium research development and design centre, Nagpur

The Centre is presently involved in tackling a number of projects related to bauxite characterisation, development of standard reference material for bauxites, improvement of digestion efficiency and precipitation characteristic in Bayer process, characterisation and utilisation of spent pot lining and other waste material resulting from the manufacture of alumina and aluminium. Besides, work on characterisation of carbonaceous materials and generation of basic process parameters for detailed engineering of specific alumina plants is in progress. The Centre is also offering consultancy services to the plants in tackling their routine problems. Discussion is in progress with TIFAC in developing a research consortium approach for VISION 2020 in the area of aluminium.

The following projects were in progress during the year:

1) Recycling :of Industrial waste into Glass

Ceramics-Building Materials Promotion Council, Ministry of Urban Development.

2) Evaluation and beneficiation of bauxite - Bombay Minerals, Jamnagar, Gujarat.

3) Evaluation of bauxite - Saurashtra Minerals, Gujarat.

4) Establishment of bauxite data bank (in collaboration with GSI).

5) Evaluation and beneficiation of low grade bauxites of Gujarat - Gujarat Mineral Development Corporation.

6) Characterisation and utilisation of spent pot lining - NALCO.

7) Characterisation of Metallurgicai grade C.P. coke ù RDCIS Ranchi.

8) Development of certified reference materials (CRM's) for bauxite - Department of Science and Technology.

Thirteen scientific papers were presented in national conferences during the course of the year.

An income of Rs.25.0 lakhs was generated upto December 31st, 1998 against the projection of Rs.40 lakhs for 1998-99.

National Institute of rock mechanics, Kolar gold field

National Institute of Rock Mechanics was registered as a society in July, 1988 to conduct research, render guidance and provide consultancy to the mining and civil engineering sectors. It has achieved excellence in the areas of (i) scientific design of mine working, (ii) design of rock excavation and support systems, and (iii) advance research in rock mechanics and ground control, This in turn, will help in improving productivity and safety in mine and civil engineering projects. The Institute has already established its expertise in the following fields :

i) rock excavation design and numerical modelling analyses,

ii) environmental geotechnical investigations,

iii) site and rock characterisation,

iv) engineering geophysics,

v) mine design,

vi) slopes stability investigations,

vii) micro-seismic investigation for ground stability evaluations,

viii) coal mine ground control,

ix) rock blasting,

x) rock mechanics instrumentation, and monitoring, and

xi) rock fracture mechanics and material tests.

Some of the major achievements in terms of technological services extended are as follows :

i) NIRM optimised the extraction from in-situ reserves in the mines of HCL, HZL and other non-coal mines;

ii) it developed tomographic imaging, PLATE-1, using the Ground Penetration Radar System for improving safety in tunneling projects; and

iii) it established Granite Mining Cell for scientific development of granite resources.

Till November, 1998, 19 sponsored projects were completed and 48 projects were ongoing, NIRM scientists published 12 research papers in international/national journals/conferences. An income of Rs. 76.64 lakhs was generated from the sponsored and S&T Projects.

National Institute of miners' health, Kolar gold field

National Institute of Miners' Health was registered as an autonomous society in February, 1990 to address exclusively the occupational health hazards/problems of miners due to their long exposures to the mining environment. In 1997-98, the Institute generated income of Rs. 1.38 lakhs from the sponsored projects. During 1998-99, up to the end of November, 1998, cash flow was of Rs. 2.63 lakhs from five completed sponsored projects.

Ongoing S&T projects

Seventeen projects are presently under implementation and one project was completed. Six new proposals have been received for consideration by the Standing Scientific Advisory Group in its next meeting.

Some of the most important projects are described hereunder:

Setting-up of technology-proving plant for nickel extraction - Hindustan Zinc Limited (HZL) and regional research laboratory (RRL), Bhubaneswar

Minister for Steel & Mines laid the foundation stone at RRL, Bhubaneswar on the 7th September, 1998 for the technology-proving plant for extraction of nickel utilising chromite overburden of Sukinda Valley. The project cost of Rs. 10.00 crores will be shared equally by HZL and CSIR. Orissa Mining Corporation will provide ore free of cost. The detailed engineering work is in progress by the turn key contractor, M/s Enfab, Secunderabad. For multi-hearth furnace, two sets of drawings have been received from Del Monego, Italy.

Development of indigenous column floatation technology

The Department of Mines, the Department of S&T and HZL have, in collaboration, commissioned two columns on 18th June, 1998 at Rajpura-Dariba mines of HZL. The significant achievement of this project is enhancement of recovery -of zinc in concentrate from 49% to 54%, reduction of insolubles from 7.5% to 2.7% and energy conservation at the rate of 2KWH/tonnes.

Performance evaluation of water injection cyclone for classification of particle - RRL, Bhopal :

The objective of the project is to carry out classification studies on water injection cyclone facility at the apex and to compare its performance with conventional hydro-cyclone for enhancing classification. The performance of a hydro-cyclone with a truncated cone and water injection facility at its apex has been studied. The preliminary results, by using water and silica as feed, show that the fines in the underflow of the cyclone can be reduced with water injection. Further experiments are in progress.

Development of cost and energy effective materials for mining industries

This project has been undertaken by RRL, Bhopal. The objectives of the project are as follows :

Development of aluminium - hard particle composites

With a view to improving the performance of cyclone parts like Refrax Apex Insert, vortex finder and inlet of slurry pumps, aluminium alloy hard particle composites have been synthesized in the laboratory as a probable substitute material for presently used cast iron lined with gum rubber. The composites have been subjected to erosion-corrosion tests in a slurry of synthetic mine water containing varying weight per cent of sand (2060%). It has been observed that wear rate increases with speed of rotation, radial distance, angle of inclination and sand content in the medium. Technical details and drawings of inlet in Sala Pumps and insert of Refrax Apex of cyclone D15 at Rampura - Agucha mines of HZL were collected. The fabrication of prototype components is in progress.

Substitution of conventional bearing bronzes with less expensive SLIZ alloys

With a view to developing effective substitute materials for the conventional bronzes for bush bearing application, various compositions of SLIZ alloys have been prepared by foundry technique. Properties of the alloys have been evaluated and compared with bronzes. It has been observed that the developed alloys exhibit reduced density and superior mechanical properties compared to lead-tin-bronzes. Alloying with nickel led to better wear properties of the SLIZ alloys at higher speeds/pressures than without this element. Based on the technical details and drawings collected from Rampura-Agucha Mines of Hindustan Zinc Ltd., prototype bushes for reciprocating feeders have been fabricated and sent for evaluation.

To develop high performance grinding balls

Grinding balls from Rampura Agucha and Zawar mines of Hindustan Zinc Ltd. have been collected and analyzed for chemical composition, micro-structure, phase analysis, hardness, abrasive wear, and erosion-corrosion properties, for developing required specifications for alternate grinding media.

Bauxite technical data/information bank -JNARDDC

In collaboration with GSI, JNARDDC is to prepare an information system and data bank for laterites and bauxites of the country, highlighting the main characteristics and technology features so that a ready reference is available to the industry. A total of 445 sheets of Maharashtra and 136 sheets of Madhya Pradesh have been entered in the computer data base with additional information acquired during investigation. About 370 samples were jointly collected out of which 265 samples have already been analysed for chemical, quantitative mineralogy and technical tests. Data is being compiled.

The work carried out so far indicates that laterites along parts of coastal Maharashtra and Koyna Valley deserve re-examination. Twenty years ago the bauxite occurrences in these areas were termed as low grade and further exploration was abandoned. Bauxite in these areas is gibbsitic with low silica content and though low in grade the ore (Al 2 0 3 : 35-40%) may be accepted for alumina production. In Madhya Pradesh the characterisation work indicates significant presence of boehmite and diaspore (mainly in Baster bauxite). Some of the bauxite samples used in cement industry are in fact found suitable for metallurgical use. The present re-evaluation may convert several laterite occurrences into bauxite deposits.

Extraction of magnesium from indigenous raw material - national metallurgical laboratory (NML), Jamshedpur

The project was approved at a cost of Rs.229 lakhs to develop indigenously a slico-thermic reduction process for magnesium production on the lines of magne-therm process. The equipment procurement has been initiated.

Study of pollution levels in asbestos mines and processing plants and to suggest appropriate mitigation measures -IBM, Nagpur

The project was approved at a cost of Rs.19 lakhs to suggest appropriate mitigation measures to reduce health hazards. Reconnoitry visits to asbestos mines and processing plants in Ajmer and Udaipur regions were carried out and 15 mines/processing plants in each region have been selected for study.

Studies on production of alloyed pig iron and low alloy steel/stainless steel using chromite overburden- MECON, Ranchi

In order to utilise the chromite overburden, which is causing environmental pollution, and to conserve nickel, chromium and cobalt resources, a process is proposed to be developed at a cost of Rs.90 lakhs to produce alloyed pig iron directly from Chromite Overburden (COB). The overburden would be beneficiated by the National Mineral Development Corporation at Hyderabad and pig iron would be produced from the concentrate at Kalinga Iron Works, Barbil, Orissa. Subsequently, the alloyed pig iron would be converted into stainless steel/low alloyed steel at Bhadravati. The Department of Science and Technology will finance 25% of the total cost.

Development of underground mining technique for lime-stone mining in western Himalayan region Central Mining Research Institute, Roorkee :

The project was approved at a cost of Rs. 16.5 lakhs to develop appropriate technology for exploitation of lime-stone reserves by underground mining technique in ecologically - fragile ground conditions. At present, lime-stone mining in the Himalayan region has been banned for ecological degradation.

12

International Co-operation

International co-operation continued to be a thrust area in the Department of Mines during the year 1998-99. Concerted and continued efforts were made to project the mineral sector as an attractive investment destination. The International Co-operation Section of the Department played an active role in achieving this goal, the key objectives being to further strengthen areas of bilateral co-operation with countries where bilateral agreements already exist, and also to enter into fresh agreements with countries which are technologically advanced, and to offer India's assistance in developing the mineral resources of other countries. Attracting foreign direct investment and facilitating inflow of state-of-the-art technologies, was another area where emphasis was laid. During the year 1998-99, the Foreign Investment Promotion Board approved 12 proposals involving Foreign Direct Investment to the tune of Rs. 474 crores in the mining sector.

Indo-French working group on mineral exploration and development

The 12th Meeting of the Indo-French Working Group on Mineral Exploration and Development was held in Paris on 7-8 October, 1998. The meeting reviewed the progress of on-going projects, and expressed satisfaction at the pace at which the projects and programmes were moving. The meeting also discussed new project proposals and prioritised the following five projects for consideration under the Indo-French Financial Protocol: (1) Impact Assessment of Mining Activities in the Subarnarekha River Basin (Geological Survey of India); (2) Pilot Project for strengthening Natural Hazard Assessment in India (Geological Survey of India); (3) Supply of one Electron Probe Microanalyser (EPMA) to Geological Survey of India; (4) Supply of laboratory equipment to Indian Bureau of Mines; and (5) Transfer of know-how for the assessment and economic evaluation of the mineral potential of Kerala State. The estimated cost of these Projects is about FF 49 million.

The 12th Meeting of the Indo-French Working Group on Mineral Exploration and Development concluded with the signing of a Protocol between the Secretary, Department of Mines and the Director General, Energy and Raw Materials, State Secretariat of Industry, Ministry of Economy, Finance & Industry, Government of France on the 8th October, 1998.

Indo-South African co-operation

South Africa is one of the major mineral producing and exporting countries in the world, with the largest known reserves of gold, chromium, platinum and vanadium. The country also has substantial deposits of minerals like coal, uranium, diamonds, iron, zirconium, titanium, felspar, nickel, phosphates, etc. South Africa has an impressive track record of mineral development and holds great potential for meaningful and mutually beneficial cooperation in the mineral sector. Ever since diplomatic ties with South Africa have been established in November, 1993, the Department of Mines has been exploring the possibility of co-operation with South Africa as both countries have some geological similarities.

India and South Africa entered into an Agreement for co-operation in the field of Geology and Mineral Resources on the 7th October, 1997. For the implementation of this Agreement, a Joint Working Group was formed, and the First Meeting of the Working Group was held at Johannesburg, South Africa in August 1998. At the end of the Working Group Meeting, a Protocol was signed in Cape Town on the 18th August, 1998, identifying six projects for mutual cooperation. Secretary, Department of Mines signed the Protocol on behalf of the Indian side, while the Director General, Department of Minerals and Energy signed on behalf of the South African side. The six projects identified for co-operation are: (1) Establishment of a detailed correlation on a formation level between the Karoo sequences in Southern Africa and the Gondwana sequences in India; (2) Geoscience Mapping in the near-shore environment along the eastern Indian coastal margin for the purpose of identifying off-shore diamond deposits; (3) Development of a pre-Gondwana precambrian crustal evolution and metallogenic map for India and Southern Africa; (4) Evaluation of stability of underground mine workings through micro-seismic techniques; (5) Hydro-fracturing for street measurement; and (6) Characterisation and processing of gold, diamond and platinum group of metal ores and to evolve suitable beneficiation processes. With the signing of the Protocol, a beginning has been made for a long and fruitful cooperation between the two countries in the field of geology and mineral resources.

The South African Deputy Minister for Minerals & Energy, Ms Susan Shabhangu, accompanied by a seven member delegation, visited India on the invitation of the Minister of State for Steel & Mines from 27th to 31st October, 1998. The Hon'ble Minister visited the Indian Mining Machinery Exhibition (IMME) '98 at New Delhi and also addressed the Mining Summit.

Vietnam

The Department of Mines and Public Sector Undertakings participated in the 2nd 'Pride of India' Exhibition organised from 23rd to 26th, October, 1998 at Hanoi, Vietnam. The Indian delegation for the Exhibition held encouraging discussions with the Vietnamese authorities and company representatives on enhancing co-operation between the two countries in the mineral sector. Discussion was also held with the Vietnamese authorities from the Pac Lang Gold Joint Venture Project between Hindustan Zinc Limited, LaSource, France and VMC, Vietnam.

Russia

The fifth session of the Indo-Russian Working Group on Ferrous and Non-Ferrous Metallurgy was held in Moscow, Russia on 24-25 November, 1998. The meeting reviewed the progress on bilateral co-operation in the areas identified by earlier Working Group meetings such as technology transfers in copper, zinc and aluminium industries.

Myanmar

The Department of Mines was represented in the Indian delegation which visited Myanmar in October 1998, for bilateral talks for enhancing trade and economic co-operation between India and Myanmar. In the mineral sector cross border co-operation along the Manipur/Mizoram border has been identified as an area of mutual interest.